# POP-CULT

®

©

## PUBLISHING

Since 1977

nart@fastcheapandeasy.com

Fast, Cheap & Easy
Graphics

Produced by Pop-Cult Publishing in cooperation with
Fast, Cheap & Easy Graphics

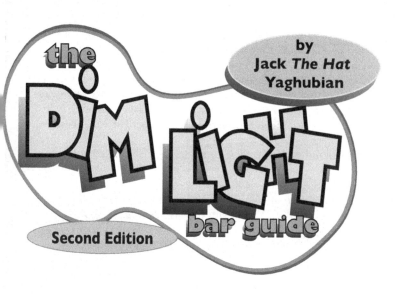

the DIM LIGHT bar guide

by Jack *The Hat* Yaghubian

Second Edition

**Now 20% more scathing**

1288 Columbus Ave. #179, San Francisco, California 94133
jack@fastcheapandeasy.com
Second Edition  Version 1.4.8.
*the Dim Light bar guide/Second Edition/*Jack Yaghubian 1949—
Other books by Jack Yaghubian: *Grunt's Minutia, the Dim Light bar guide Volume One*

Available from City Lights Boostore, San Francisco and wherever such fine products are sold.

**Credits**:
Cover art, and book design by Fast, Cheap & Easy Graphics.
Many of the illustrations are based on photos taken by Tony Velour, the one on page 139 is from a photo taken by Catalina Orrego, the rest are based on photos by the author.

**Acknowledgements:**
I would like to thank my editors, Joanna Lioce and Jessica Loos and the many bartenders and cocktail waitresses I have worked with and/or known since I began bartending in 1986. All of these people and those who bought the original version of *the Dim Light bar guide*, helped to make the completion of *the Dim Light bar guide/Second Edition* possible.

Special thanks to Richard C. Leto, who gave me the idea to begin work on the original version of this book and who also gave me a tip on how to proceed. While his advice was invaluable, sadly, his abilities fall short in the board game of *Risk*.

"Everything I viewed as a perk
when I first became a bartender,
I now recognize as an occupational hazard."

—Jack *The Hat* Yaghubian

Everyone here brings joy;

some by entering,

some by leaving.

# Table of Contents

The author in a moment of quiet
reflexion.

# Author's Note

SIXTEEN YEARS AGO, as I sat down to write the author's note for *the Dim Light bar guide, Volume I* I was on a mission to educate the drinking public: The weekend warriors, the V.I.P.s, the Princes and Princesses, and the twelve year olds, all of whom make bartending trying at times. Since then I've been disillusioned; the people who bought and read *the Dim Light bar guide* were bartenders and bar regulars; people who knew the material as well or better than me. In other words, I failed. This knowledge caused me to stop and take stock: "Hey,... I'm preaching to the choir!"

With that revelation came the understanding that there was no need to tread so lightly on my subject matter. For instance, the original working title was *the Dim Bulb bar guide*. But as publication day drew near, in late 1998, I decided I shouldn't insult the very people I was trying to reach, so I toned it down to *the Dim Light bar guide*. At this point it's sixteen years too late to go back to that original title. However, I can say, unequivocally, that this second edition of *the Dim Light bar guide* is indeed twenty percent more scathing than the first, and while it's written with the dim bulbs in mind, it's written for the drinking professionals. I hope you like it.

Jack Yaghubian, July 2014 San Francisco, CA

Note: With changes in the bar industry since *the Dim Light bar guide, Volume I* was first published, this edition has been expanded and updated, graphics have been changed and the book has been completely redesigned. I have also added three new chapters: Credit Cards, Beer Snobbery and Mixology. For those familiar with the first edition, this is not volume two, which was to be about life as a bartender. This is the second edition of the first volume. Plans for volume two were scraped shortly after work began on it and there are currently no plans to revive the project.

# BARTENDERS ARE JUST LEGAL DRUG DEALERS

# Ordering and Paying

**O**RDERING A DRINK AND PAYING FOR IT may seem second nature, but a bar is different than the average retail establishment. In a way a bar is like a sweat shop in that it's essentially piece work; the more pieces of work a member of the bar staff completes per hour, the more money he or she makes. This being the case, efficiency is the essence of bar work. The staff of any bar tends to be efficient, but not so the customers. There are those that know what their doing and those that haven't a clue. It's the latter who slow things down for everyone and it's this group to which the following is addressed.

•**KNOW WHAT YOU WANT BEFORE YOU GET THE BARTENDER'S ATTENTION** This is especially important when the bar is very busy or *slammed*.

•**WHEN WITH A GROUP DESIGNATE ONE PERSON TO BOTH ORDER AND PAY** No bartender wants to have five people come up to the bar and have to deal with them one at a time when he could deal with them as a group. An added advantage to this method of ordering is that you can tip less per drink, especially if the drinks you order are simple and particularly if they are all the same—bartenders expect a larger percentage on complex drinks ordered individually. If you insist on paying with plastic, don't break it up into separate tabs; have one person put it all on their card and figure it out between yourselves later. Splitting credit card tabs looks cheap and wastes the time of both the bartender and other customers waiting to be served.

•**DON'T STRING-ORDER** Bartenders don't like being treated like a yo-yo. Give your entire order at once, don't break it up into a string of mini-orders so the bartender thinks she's done, when you have additional drinks to order. This applies if you have opened a tab with your card. Don't keep ordering drinks one at a time as you need them, order in rounds.

•**YOU DON'T HAVE THE BARTENDER ON A LEASH** Just because you have the bartender's attention that doesn't mean he's yours. If you don't have an order ready, he'll move on if there's other business at hand. And again, this goes for open tabs—he's not on a leash just because you have an open tab. Sending one person after another up to the bar to get individual drinks charged to your card will get you on his bad side.

•**NAME BOOZE FIRST WHEN ORDERING** For instance, a vodka-cranberry rather than cranberry-vodka. This will speed up the process by giving the bartender information in the order of importance. In this case, vodka immediately narrows your order down to vodka drinks in the bartender's mind. Cranberry pinpoints what you want. In this way you will also avoid confusion with cranberry infused vodka.

If you want your drink tall mention this first, *Tall* vodka-cranberry. If you don't the bartender may have already filled a highball glass with ice and will have to start over.

•**SPECIFY VARIATIONS** For example, a vodka martini. A martini is gin and vermouth chilled, served in an up glass with olives. Many people order a martini when what they really want is a vodka martini. Most bartenders will ask to be sure, since vodka martinis are common, but if you order a martini and the bartender starts to work without asking your preference, you can expect gin.

In recent years, due to the work of advertising agencies in the employ of large distilleries, there has been a proliferation of up-drinks that liquor advertisements call martinis. They are not martinis, but like martinis, they are up drinks and are served in a martini glass. They include things like Cosmopolitans and Lemon Drops but have expanded to include all sorts of fru fru drinks that are served up. These are the drinks most often ordered by the weekend crowd who think they are being sophisticated, but they are wrong. Ordering these drinks just shows people that you are an unsophisticated drinker who is easily manipulated by the media, so do yourself and your bartender a favor and stop calling them martinis.

On the other hand, it could be argued that since anything that comes in a highball glass is called a highball, it would follow that drinks served in a martini glass would be called martinis. I disagree, and here's why: The original Highball was whiskey and ginger ale. The glass it was served in had to be big enough to accommodate the booze, ice and mixer. Eventually highball came to mean any drink that consisted of booze, ice and mixer and was served in a highball glass. Other than capitalizing the *H*, there's no difference in terminology between the specific drink and a whole family of drinks. However, when someone orders a highball they never say, "I'd like a screwdriver highball," they simply ask for a screwdriver. The same then holds for up drinks. There's no reason to ask for a Lemon Drop martini, Lemon Drop is enough. Two exceptions I can think of are a vodka martini and a chocolate martini because there's no other name for them.

•**CALL LIQUOR** If you want a screwdriver made with Stoli, say so up front, "I want a Stoli screwdriver." Occasionally a customer has watched me pour a screwdriver and then asked, "Don't you have Stoli?" Of course I have Stoli, but if you don't ask for it I will make the drink with well booze.

•**SPECIAL INSTRUCTIONS** Occasionally a customer will order a custom-made drink or a drink so far out of the ordinary that few people have ever heard of it. These drinks are usually ordered by amateur mixologists or by people who found a recipe in an old Playboy. If the bar isn't busy and you know what you're doing this is fine, but anticipate some variation from what you're expecting.

People who order these drinks often start by telling the bartender the amounts: "Three shots of gin, a shot of Kahlúa, a shot of Chambord," etc. Customers who do this don't know what they're talking about and end up describing a drink that would fill a pint glass and cost a small fortune.

The way to order special drinks is by parts per ingredient: "Three parts gin, one part Kahlúa, one part Chambord, chilled, up with a cherry." This tells the bartender everything she needs to know: It's a drink based on gin with the flavors of coffee and raspberry, chilled, then strained into an up glass and garnished with a cherry… And that she's dealing with a weekend warrior.

The way not to order one of these speciality drinks is to approach the bartender, shove your smart phone in her face with the recipe brought up on the display and ask, "Will you make this for me?" I was in a local bar and was told that this happened to one of the seasoned bartenders on the staff. Her response was, "Put down your phone and order a drink." I guess she was in a good mood that night.

•**HAVE A SECOND CHOICE** If you have only the vaguest idea of the ingredients, it's better to order something else. In such cases the bartender can only go by your description. If it sounds really odd, the bartender will tell you, but since the advent of mixology there seems to be no limit to the abominations people will conceive of, then foist upon a gullible public. And remember, once the drink is made, that's it. Some bartenders will replace it if you don't like it, but then you've wasted their time and the boss's booze. Others will tell you, "Hey, that's what you asked for," and they'll move on to the next customer.

The fact is, no bartender knows all the drinks in all the books, not to mention the ones that are of recent invention and not published. Another fact is that it's not to a bartender's financial advantage to know more than a small fraction of all the possible drinks, because few people are going to order them. Those who do order drinks that are way out of the norm are usually people who don't go to bars very often, which means they probably don't tip very well, if at all. Bartenders have little incentive to remember an obscure drink recipe or look it up in a recipe book, combine all the ingredients, then try to figure out what to charge. If it's really slow and there's no other work to do it can be a diversion, but that's the best that can be said on the subject.

•**DON'T PLACE YOUR ORDER, THEN WALK AWAY** The bartender can usually produce the drinks faster than you think and will be standing there wondering where you've gone by the time you return from the restroom or talking with friends. As soon as you place your order you should be reaching for your wallet, if your money isn't already out. This also goes for ordering from a server, stay where you were when you placed your order so she doesn't have to go in search of you.

•**PLACING A LARGE ORDER** Don't start picking up drinks and ferrying them to your friends before the bartender has completed your order, unless you first ask her if it's okay to do so. Generally, the bartender will add your bill in her head as she completes your order, but if you have a large group or if she's distracted she may lose track. If she does and the drinks are spread around the barroom in the hands of your friends, she will have no choice other than to estimate your bill, and it won't be in your favor.

•**HAVE YOUR MONEY OUT WHEN THE DRINKS ARRIVE** This may be sooner than you think, so it's best to have your money ready at the time you order.

•**PAY WITH THE LARGEST BILL OR COMBINATION OF BILLS THAT WILL COVER THE ORDER** Don't wait until the bartender tells you what you owe and then start looking through every bill in your wallet for the closest combination of bills.

•**DON'T TOSS A CRUMPLED PILE OF BILLS ON THE BAR AS YOUR PAYMENT**

•**AVOID USING COINS** Tip with coins only if you received them in change from the bartender. Increasingly, bars are pricing their drinks in whole dollar amounts and have little or no use for coin.

•**CASH IS BETTER THAN PLASTIC** Credit card transactions are slow and they cost the owner, the bartender and you money. Cash is fast and efficient, plastic is slow and inefficient (see **CREDIT CARDS**).

•**CHECKS** Bars don't take them.

•**TRAVELER'S CHECKS** Few people use them anymore and increasingly, bars won't accept them. In fact many of the younger bar workers aren't even sure what a traveler's check is. If you have them, cash them at the bank and use real cash in a bar.

•**REGIONAL DIFFERENCES** While on vacation it's good to keep in mind that different regions of the country and the world have different tastes. What's preferred in some regions will be rare or unknown in others.

For instance, I've had Spanish customers order red wine and Coke. Argentines like Fernet and coke served as a highball. When Europeans order a martini, what they are probably expecting is Martini & Rossi Vermouth on the rocks, although Some Englishmen like 7-Up in their beer (Chandies and Lager Tops). Americans from the Mid-west like tomato juice in their beer (Red Beer). Over the years that I've bartended in San Francisco, Canadians and people from the Northeastern U.S., have occasionally ordered Caesars. A Caesar is a Bloody Mary made with Clamato juice. However, bars in San Francisco don't carry Clamato juice.

Some people like their stout at room temperature, others like a lemon wedge in their wheat beer. These people are Americans who have been to Europe. While I assume they exist, I have never encountered an Irish customer who asked me for warm stout or complained that his Guinness was too cold. When I have offered a lemon wedge in wheat beer to Germans or Belgians, nine times out of ten they have declined it, often with a puzzled look in my direction.

There are also variations in the names of drinks. For instance, I recently met a Dutchman who told me *Jager Bombs* are called *Flying Deers* in the Netherlands.

•YOU CAN JUDGE BOOZE BY ITS BOTTLE As a rule of thumb, the plainer the bottle, the simpler the label and the more unfamiliar the name, the better the booze it contains. For instance, when confronted by an array of scotch bottles, the ones you recognize and ones that you've never seen, the unfamiliar bottle is probably the better of the group. However, I would recommend asking the price before ordering it.

Also, it's best to avoid bottles shaped like people or animals, that look as if they were specially designed to stand out on the shelf, or that come in anything other than clear, green, or brown glass bottles with paper labels. If you order top shelf vodka that comes in a bottle which has been frosted and silk-screened, you're paying for the bottle.

N'art? is the question.

If you want to see the future
imagine the invisible hand of
the market place punching
a human face
forever.

# Cash is still King

**B**ARS WERE AMONG THE LAST BASTIONS of *Cash Only* retail. Credit cards began to erode this situation about twenty years ago and as they did, the income of bartenders eroded as well. Today bartenders make less than they did twenty years ago. Bankers, on the other hand, make far more than they did twenty years ago. For this reason alone I despise credit cards. But there's more to it than just my own bottom line.

When I voice my dislike of credit cards I'm often told that they're the wave of the future (even though they've been around since mid-20th century). But by definition the future is that which has yet to arrive, currently cash is still the simpler, more efficient way to pay in a bar. And there are other payment methods, such as paying with your smart phone, that are more modern than credit cards. And Segways are more modern than bicycles, but which gets you where you're going more efficiently?

Credit cards, on the other hand, are slow and laborious. If you've worked in retail you know this. I've been slowed by credit cards since the late 60s when I worked in the men's and boy's bargain basement at the May Company. When people say newer credit cards systems are faster, they're right—faster than the old systems, but slower than cash. Have you ever noticed that the line slows down whenever someone pulls out a credit card? People who use credit cards in bars or other high volume retail settings are the modern equivalent of the old lady in a long checkout line at the supermarket who insists on paying by check.

## •PAYING WITH CASH

When a customer pays in cash, I ring it in, hand them their change, put the tip in my tip jar and move on.

## •PAYING WITH A CREDIT CARD

When they pay with a card I ring it in, then go through a separate process with the credit card machine. One feature of these machines is that they tend to slow down when their system is busy, which is usually Friday and Saturday nights—The machine gets slower when the bar is at its busiest. I won't record here what goes through my mind when I'm in the middle of a slammed Saturday night shift and the little machine next to the register is telling me, "dialing now... dialing now... dialing now... authenticating... authenticating... authenticating."

A minor concern, but still a concern, is stolen credit cards. Unless the bartender confirms each card when the tab is opened, he could be dealing with a stolen card. The bartender's choice is to take the time to confirm the card or take the chance that at the end of the night the he will be left holding a bad card, against which the customer has rung up a tab and then walked.

Far more often, customers will forget that they have a card open and walk out without closing it. Every bar I've worked in that takes plastic has wads of forgotten cards laying around.

Then there's the matter of keeping track of open tabs. First I must write the name of the customer on a slip of paper, record what he has been served, then wrap the paper around his card and put it on the register. If I'm dealing with three cards or less it's just an annoyance, but when it reaches five or six cards it becomes a problem. Finding the right card to record subsequently ordered drinks costs me several seconds each time a drink is added to a tab. In a slammed bar a few seconds delay, here and there, creates a swimming-in-glue effect, costing the bar and myself time when time is at a premium.

And when it comes time to close a tab other problems arise. Customers will often open their tab at the bar, but eventually they move to a table and their tab is transferred to the wait staff. From the bartender's perspective this represents a loss of income in the form of lost tips, of which he will get a small percentage when the wait staff tips him out at the end of the shift. It also presents another problem when the customer comes back to the bar, where she opened her tab, and now wants to close it. At this point I no longer have her card, the waitress does. So now I have to find the waitress.

People often want to close out their tab when it isn't convenient for me because I'm busy. Customers become impatient when they want to go and don't seem to understand that, when timeliness is a concern, cash is the faster option. When they complain, "You know, I really have to be somewhere, now," I point out that had they paid with cash, they would already be walking down the street.

Then there's the joker that informs the bartender or the waitress that they are still holding his card, even though he has already settled his bill. This usually initiates a frantic search for a card dropped in the speed rack or some other location behind the bar. It almost always ends with the customer exclaiming, "Oh never mind, I found it! It was in my front pocket." Douche.

Far worse are the times the customer wants to close out his tab but a member of the bar staff has gotten cards mixed up and another customer has walked out with the wrong card. Ouch!

Yet another drawback to running tabs is that it is sometimes necessary to cut a customer off. Not all customers take this well. Those who don't tend to become agitated. If an agitated customer has a tab open, the process of ejecting him is further complicated. Plus, in most bars the bartender has to turn his back to run the tab and is put in the uncomfortable position of standing with his back to a customer who is making insulting and/or threatening comments. "...Dialing now... dialing now... dialing now..."

Then there's the matter of credit card minimums; bars set a minimum amount for credit card transactions because the banks take, on average, 3 percent of the gross sale. They also charge a flat transaction fee of 30 cents every time a card is swiped. You can see how the percent of profit taken by banks rises in transactions under ten dollars, when the 30 cent transaction fee alone is 3 percent of gross sale. At ten dollars the banks take 6 percent of the gross sale. Keeping in mind that profit is a fraction of the gross, the percentage of the bar's profit the banks take is far higher than 6 percent. This is why ten dollars is generally the lowest credit card minimum you will find in a bar. The bar's profit shrinks to nothing as a credit card sale falls below ten dollars. People don't understand this. Some will even tell you minimums are against the law! If there is such a law, it's the banker's law. By breaking their law the only punishment one could possibly incur is that the bank can revoke your credit card machine. But of course they would never do that because they want your money, so who cares what their law is?

Often, when a customer encounters the bar's minimum, they will actually buy more than they want just to reach that minimum.

Some will actually ask you to charge them more for their drink, so they will reach the minimum. Why would anyone ask to pay more for anything in any situation? Equally puzzling is that people who use credit cards often have cash visible in their wallets. They have cash, but they insist on paying with their card, even though cash would be faster, cheaper and easier.

And from the bartender's perspective there is another big negative to plastic transactions: There is no way to know if they are dealing with a stiff when they run a tab. This puts the bartender in the position of a waiter in a restaurant who has far fewer, but far larger transactions per shift. Have you ever noticed that bartenders are more forthright than waiters? This is because to a waiter one transaction may be ten percent of his night's income. He has to be very attentive and agreeable in order to maximize his chances of getting a good tip when a table has finished. The dynamic of the bar is altered when a bartender opens a tab and he's put in the same position as a waiter.

Finally, I have to adjust the tip, which means I have to stop bartending and start inputting information into the little credit card machine. And it doesn't end there; after closing time I have to print out the report and put all of the little credit card slips in order, else suffer the wrath of management.

When I've talked to customers about their use of credit cards a few have told me, "I'm afraid of getting mugged. Credit cards are safer." This is another false concept spread by bankers. Why would anyone feel that they're less likely to be mugged if they carry credit cards? Besides, every time you use one the bankers are taking a bit of your money, either directly or indirectly, so by using them you're guaranteed to be robbed, even if only by a small amount, every single time. There's no need to go into the fraudulent use of stolen credit cards and thieves getting access to your account numbers, because it's in the news all of the time. "But I have theft protection." Really? And who pays for that? The banks? No. They just spread their loss, in the form of higher fees, among their customers.

And finally there's the credit card customers, who when asked, tell you that they don't have any cash, usually with an air of smugness. It's as if carrying no cash makes them one of the special people. And they are special people, special to the bankers whom they are enriching.

•**POINTS** People seem to believe they receive extra value, when using their credit card instead of cash, because of the points they receive for using their credit cards. My how generous the credit card companies are! This just shows how gullible the public is. Sure the credit card companies give you a nickel here and a nickel there, but that's because they're taking a dime here and a dime there. Credit cards are a form of currency with a built-in tax on spending it.

## •TOUCH SCREEN REGISTERS

Bars run on the corporate model use expensive touch screen register systems to keep track of plastic transactions and speed up the process. I've seen some bartenders who are fast with these devices when dealing with credit cards, it's not as fast as cash, but much faster than a plastic transaction on the dial-up modem I work with. But these same devices require the bartender to push so many buttons for just about every transaction that it's a wash at best, unless most or all of your transactions are on cards, which is exactly where the bankers are leading us.

Another misunderstood function of these systems is inventory control. They do keep track of inventory, but only in a general sense. It would be foolish for a bar manager to rely only on what one of these systems told him was in inventory. In every retail setting, especially bars, there is shrinkage, e.g. booze is spilled, bottles are broken, bartenders drink it, freebees aren't recorded, one bartender has a heavier hand than another, etc. Touch screen register systems may have software to approximate shrinkage, but they can't keep an accurate accounting. The manager still has to go into the stock room and physically count the bottles, or run the risk of running out of well vodka on a Saturday night.

More to the point is an aspect of touch screen registers that's rarely mentioned; they are a form of surveillance. Every time a bar worker goes into the register they need to use a PIN number, otherwise the register won't allow them access. How long, how often and what business is conducted during those visits is recorded. This is why they first appeared in corporate structured work environments; the owners don't know their employees, don't pay or treat them well, thus they don't trust them.

So my advice, if you are one of those who never carries cash, is to stop slumming; stick to corporate bars and restaurants, those clean, shiny new ones with no character. These sorts of establishments are where you will feel the most welcome and will eventually be your only option anyway; various forms of electronic payment will eventually put old school, single location bars with involved owners out of business. The lobbying efforts of bankers, their pockets bloated with money from skimming all plastic/electronic transactions, will make sure of that. Then all bars, or more accurately, all *retail alcohol consuming establishments*, will be owned by faceless corporations and run by managers with business school degrees. And nothing says *fun* like *business school degree*. Oh boy!

(See AutoRace page 133)

cash

plastic

# ONE DOLLAR
# =
# ONE VOTE

**THE BANKS AND CORPORATIONS** have long dreamed of a future where they stand as the gate keepers in nearly every aspect of our lives. It is a future where you won't be able to have a sidewalk sale, a poker game or even loan a friend money without the banks taking a cut and keeping a digital record of the transaction. Of course, this future has yet to be fully realized. Ultimately, the power of the banks and corporations rises and falls based on how much we invest in them. The way things currently stand, where and how we spend our money is more important than who or what we vote for. *The customer is always right* mentality, with the bending, scraping and false smiles it mandates is the corporate candidate. But my preference is for the old bar down the street where the bartender knows my name and when he thinks I'm wrong or out of line, he tells me so with an honest scowl.

# Not a Good Idea to Order

•**Wine** If you're a wine connoisseur, you might want to think about ordering something else in a bar. Most bars will have a small selection and they don't take care of their wine as you would like. In my experience, wine lovers are often disappointed by the wine they get in a bar.

Occasionally I'm asked why we don't have a better selection of wine and why we open bottles before they're needed. The reason is that when someone orders a glass of wine the bartender wants to be able to pour it as quickly as possible. Rather than stopping to open a bottle when he's slammed, bartenders often open one or more bottles in advance. To answer the first question; the more choices you offer the more bottles you will have opened, and the greater the chance that someone will send the wine back because it's been open too long for their taste. Wine drinkers are just too finicky to be accommodated. You will never have a gin and tonic sent back because the gin bottle has been open too long.

The way I've come to deal with this over the years is that when a customer asks me, "Do you have a nice wine," I always say, "No, I don't." The tip-off is the word *nice*; this tells me that they're likely to be fussy, so I avoid the problem altogether. They usually appreciate this and it's good for the boss too; it does her no good for me to pour a glass of wine down the drain and replace it with a vodka tonic. I serve them the vodka tonic in the first place and save time and expense for everyone concerned.

This is beginning to change with the advent of good wine coming in bottles with screw caps. The fancy name for this type of closure is Stelvin. While screw caps have a bad reputation in the U.S., due to their being used for cheap wine from California, outside of the U.S. there is no such taint and Stelvin closures are growing in popularity. There's no need to open them until needed, which means the bottle won't be open as long before it's poured off.

•**BLOODY MARYS AFTER FIVE IN THE AFTERNOON** Bloody Marys are a morning or an afternoon drink. You can order them at night, but you're showing the bartender and the other customers that you don't know what you're doing. The only possible excuse I can think of for ordering a Bloody Mary after five in the afternoon is someone who just got off a very long flight and thinks it's morning.

•**LONG ISLAND ICED TEA** A little bit of everything, so it tastes like nothing. A drink for the college crowd, but if you're over 25, it's a bit silly. It's also a classic cheapskate drink.

•**TOP SHELF LONG ISLAND ICED TEA** Sillier yet—at twice the price.

•**FLAMING DRINKS** Lighting an alcoholic drink on fire is senseless and potentially dangerous. The alcohol is expensive and when you light a drink on fire it's the alcohol that's burning. The longer you let it burn the lower the proof of the drink. It's conceivable, if you let it burn long enough, that you could burn off all of the alcohol and end up drinking burnt water. Personally I have never lit a drink on fire; I'm of the opinion that drunks and fire don't mix. But if you insist on lighting your drink on fire, remember to smother the flame before drinking it, there's at least one example on YouTube of why you should.

•**IRISH CAR BOMB** Stupid name, stupid drink ordered by stupid people.

•**JELL-O SHOTS** Thankfully, this fad has long since ended, but things being cyclical, there's always a chance of their return.

•**WATER** Unless you're actually going to drink it, don't ask for it. I have had so many people order water over the years only to see them leave it untouched on the bar.

•**COFFEE** Bars are not cafes. Coffee is a small sideline used to wake up the bar staff, sober up the drunks and make Irish coffees and other coffee-based drinks. Because of this, bar coffee tends to be of low quality and is often stale. When the bartender makes a pot it will sit until it's finished, which may be several hours later.

For coffee drinks this is fine, because the quality of the coffee and its staleness is masked by the booze. For its other main uses, waking up staff and sobering up drunks, it will also do fine, because the former just want the caffeine and the latter are not likely to be too discriminating about the taste of their coffee. But as coffee goes, it won't be very good. If you are feeling the need for a cup of coffee as you pass a bar, it might be wise to continue down the street until you find a cafe, where they make their living selling coffee.

•**ESPRESSO** Considering the above, espresso may seem like a good idea. Many bars these days have espresso machines and since espresso is made on the spot, you know it will be fresh and relatively strong. However, you will also find that most bartenders have little interest in making espresso and probably aren't very good at it.

•**CAPPUCCINO** An even worse bet, as bartenders hate making them. The reason for this is that a cappuccino takes several times longer to make than a gin and tonic, but costs less and commands a smaller tip. Then there's the copycat order; someone sees you order a cappuccino and thinks, "Gee, that looks like a good idea," and pretty soon the bartender becomes an reluctant barista. If you want an espresso or a cappuccino, go to a cafe.

# When you snooze you lose.
# When you caffeinate you dominate.

Tired? Take a liquid nap.

# What Not to Order

•**WHAT'S GOOD HERE?** My answer is always: "Beer."

•**WHAT DO YOU LIKE?** My answer is always: "Beer."

•**WHAT'S YOUR SPECIALTY?** My answer is always: "BEER."

•**WHAT DO YOU LIKE MAKING?** My answer is always: "Beer."

•**SURPRISE ME!** People who ask me to surprise them always get beer.

•**AMATEUR HOUR DRINKS** These are drinks that tell the bartender that you don't drink very often. They include just about anything that comes out of a blender, calls for a small paper umbrella or is found on a drink menu. They also indicate to the bartender that the tip is going to be stingy.

•**FRU FRU DRINKS** Closely related to Amateur hour drinks. Generally, people ordering these drinks do spend a good deal of time in bars, they just don't like the taste of alcohol and/or aren't very sophisticated drinkers. Fru Fru drinks can be recognized by the fact that they are often sweet, call for three or more ingredients and have cute names like Alabama Slammer, Corpse Reviver, or Blue Hawaiian.

•**FAD LIQUORS** Liquors that come into fashion for a couple of years due to savvy marketing techniques. Examples are: flavored vodkas, bourbons with added sweeteners and flavors, and cheap, spiced or coconut flavored rum to lure in young drinkers and weekend warriors.

•**HOUSE SPECIALS** Usually some concoction management has dreamed up to sell to suckers; cheap booze mixed with all sorts of crap and sold at greater than normal markup. Unless, of course, you're in a mixology bar. Then it's expensive booze mixed with all sorts of crap and sold at greater than normal markup.

•**EXTRA STRONG** I have found over the years that people who ask for their drinks extra strong are cheapskates. Consequently, they get nothing extra from me. It's a simple matter to pack the glass extra tight with ice so there's less room for liquid, which will make the glass look fuller. If it's a drink that calls for mixer, a splash will fill it, so the drink will taste stronger, even though it contains no more than a shot of booze.

It's also possible to short-pour and add a float of booze at the end. This makes the customer think you're adding extra booze and when he takes his first sip it will taste strong because the float will be on top. If he stiffs me again, I simply short-pour him on his next round and add even less mixer.

•**STRONG ISLAND ICED TEA** Always a cheapskate.

•**LESS ICE** Some people will order their highballs with less ice or no ice thinking that the bartender will make up for the lost volume by adding more booze. This is a classic rookie move. The bartender will give you a half-full highball. If you complain it's not full she'll fill it with mixer, not booze.

On the other hand, some people just don't like ice in their drinks—nothing wrong with that. But again, expect the glass to appear to be less than full.

•**SHOOTERS** I don't recommend shooters. Usually sweet concoctions with naughty names so that amateurs can think that they're getting down with their bad selves. Give me a break.

•**POPPERS** Shooters plus soda pop, which are slammed on the bar top, causing them to foam. Luckily, these have gone out of fashion—for the time being.

•**ANY DRINK FOUND ON A DRINK MENU** Lists of beer, wine and spirits sold in the establishment are an obvious exception.

•**STUMPING THE BARTENDER** Some people seem to believe that if they order a drink the bartender hasn't heard of, she will be impressed with their knowledge. This simply isn't true. The impression the bartender receives from such an order is that she's dealing with a novice drinker.

•**SOMETHING REFRESHING** I recently had a customer come in, take a seat at the bar and tell me, "I like bourbon and I'd like something refreshing. I like citrus—lemon or lime." This is mixology-speak for, "I only have the vaguest idea of what I want, I'm lazy and used to being catered to by mixologists." Taking offense at being confused with a mixologist, I took my retribution on this clueless customer by serving him a neat shot of Makers Mark with both a lemon and a lime wedge on a serviette. He didn't look pleased, but he did pay up and spent the remainder of his time in my bar talking with his wife.

# FASHION COMES FROM WITHOUT, STYLE COMES FROM WITHIN.

FASHION

STYLE

## DON'T CONFUSE THE TWO.

# Mixology

**M**ODERN MIXOLOGY AROSE about twenty years ago. Since then it slowly spread across the land and has now come to dominate high-end bars and restaurants. However, few of the drinks it has introduced have been worth drinking and fewer still are worth the wait or the price. They tend to be over shaken, overly complicated and just generally over done—A waste of good booze.

When you think about it, *mixologist* is a silly, made-up word for a job done standing on your feet. When a garbage collector refers to himself as a *garbologist* he knows it's silly; he's being humorous. From what I can tell, mixologists don't see the humor. They believe they are bringing back a noble profession by resurrecting antique cocktail recipes and inventing new ones in an effort to keep the tradition alive. The problem is, it's not a tradition, it's a sign of the times.

The places that promote mixology tend to elicit the mood of two periods in American history: The Gilded Age and The Roaring Twenties. What these two periods have in common with our own age is the vast disparity in the distribution of wealth. The average Joe or Mary wasn't drinking these elaborate concoctions back in the late 1800s or in the 1920s. Jerry Thomas, considered the father of mixology, was making drinks for the robber barons and their associates—the 1% of the late 1800s. The average woman in the 1920s wasn't a flapper and she didn't drink much, if at all. What mixology represents is the decadence of our age, where everything has to be elaborate, pretentious and expensive.

A common misconception is that mixology is a mark of sophisticated drinking in times of growing sophistication. What it actually represents is unsophisticated drinking in times of growing hedonism. Alcohol is an acquired taste. What mixology does is what fru fru drinks have always done; it masks the taste of booze with sweeteners, spices, etc. for those who have yet to acquire a taste for alcohol. Then it gussies them up with flourishes, garnishes and little tricks, like igniting the oil squeezed from citrus peel in a crowd pleasing puff of fire. Related to fru fru drinks are tiki drinks, which are made for adults who rarely go out and hardly drink when they do. They are intimidated by bars in general, and aren't keen on the taste of alcohol, but in a tiki bar they can have a sweet, fruity cocktail in a safe environment. Tiki and fru fru drinks are the choice of unsophisticated drinkers and it's with tiki and fru fru drinks that mixology drinks are rightly categorized.

It's no secret that in mixology bars (A.K.A. *cocktail bars,* in which the person making drinks would be called a *cocktologist*), even though they are always over-staffed, it takes forever to get a drink. I've been told by more than one person that when they have been to such places they tend to order their drinks two at a time to cut down on the wait between rounds.

If you go into one of these establishments what you won't see is a collection of locals relaxing after work. What you won't hear is an exchange of ideas between the mixologist and his customers. What you will see is a room full of people with money to burn: Suits, techies, hipsters, hopsters and vacationers (drinkologists, I suppose).

What you will hear is a lot of talk about the drink being made: The history of the drink, the expensive, exotic tinctures and elixirs used to make the drink, but not a word is uttered concerning religion, sex or politics.

It seems mixologists are on a mission to talk customers out of what they want and into something more complicated and exotic. This is fine when they're dealing with amateurs who have no idea of what they want, but it can be counter productive when it comes to veteran drinkers. A regular of mine related to me that he recently stopped into a mixology bar with an English friend. It was a warm day and his friend asked the mixologist for a Pimms and soda. The mixologist told him that what he really wanted was a Pimms Cup, which also contained gin and was mixed with ginger beer, not soda. The English-man was in his fifties and had been drinking Pimms and soda since he was a teenager, but the twenty-something American mixologist felt it was his duty to educate him. After leaving the bar the English visitor commented that he would have preferred a Pimms and soda. Sometimes you don't want something better. Sometimes you just want what you want. And sometimes something *better* isn't.

An annoying hallmark of mixology is that the mixologist precisely measures every primary ingredient. Precisely measuring ingredients may be necessary in baking, is generally unnecessary in cooking, and has no place in a bar. Precisely measuring ingredients is part of the show and is meant to give the impression of quality. But it's just a show. What it actually represents is a focus on the bottom line.

Another practice of the mixologists is that he samples every drink he makes with a straw. He wants to give the impression that he's a liquid chef, taste testing each glass before it's served—Quality control. I don't recall ever seeing a mixologist make a correction to a drink after tasting it, but that's not the point, again, it's just part of the show.

This leads me to an observation made by a friend of mine. He believes the proliferation of mixologists in recent years is due to the growth in popularity of culinary academies. With a brand new degree (that costs a minimum of twenty-thousand dollars) a culinary academy graduate qualifies for a job as a line cook making about twelve bucks an hour. If he is lucky enough to find that job, he faces a life of long hours in a hot kitchen standing on his feet, getting burns and cuts, all for a paltry paycheck at the end of the pay period.

While so employed he is introduced to the bartenders who work the front of the house. They get paid less per hour, but with tips they far out-strip his hourly wage on the cooking line. It can't take long for the new line cook to realize he can pay off his student debt faster while enjoying a better social life if he just moved to the front of the house. However, those that manage to make that move find they are frustrated by being unable to use the knowledge they acquired at such great expense. Thus a mixologist is born.

Perhaps the most ridiculous display I've seen, in the realm of mixology, was at a high-end Japanese steak house that had recently opened. I took a seat at the bar and ordered a beer. Behind the bar was a huge, crystal clear block of ice which was under-lit so that it glowed in the darkened interior of the bar. Soon a bar-back in a white jacket appeared and began to saw the block of ice with a steel ice saw. He was cutting a slab about 1-½" thick. I asked a woman seated next to me if that's what they served the sushi on. "Oh, no. He's making ice cubes for the drinks," she replied.

On a subsequent visit I overheard a conversation between the bartender and a customer; the customer was asking the bartender to clarify his bill. He had been drinking bourbon on the rocks and apparently they charged him extra for the hand cut ice cubes! Can it get any more pretentious than artisanal ice cubes? I bet it can and will.

These are places where people go to exhibit conspicuous consumption; all pretense with none of the civilizing features found in a bar. Jerry Thomas was famous for inventing the Blue Blazer, a drink that he lit on fire, then poured between two mixing vessels, blue flame following the arc of liquid between the vessels. He was a showman, putting on a show for wealthy people. When you light alcohol on fire you're burning what you paid for, not all that different from lighting your cigar with a burning dollar bill.

Mixology bars are created by monied investors, run by front men and will last until the investors feel it's time to cash out. The crowd they attract is fickle, always looking for the next new trend. Mixology bars are not places that will stand the test of time, these are not the institutions of tomorrow. They are now found in virtually every city in the nation and are spreading to the suburbs… it's everywhere. As was the case with grappa in the 80s, cigars in the 90s, and juggling bartenders after the release of the movie *Cocktail*, this trend will begin to deteriorate when there's nowhere else for it to go and the public turns its attention elsewhere.

I recently served a customer who told me she was 84 years old. She went on to tell me that in the 1950s tiki bars were the big thing. "Zombies were the drink, they were everywhere. But when they were done, they were done. They disappeared over night."

Mixology has reached it's limits and will soon begin to fade away. Some of the drinks, in simplified form, will be incorporated into general bar offerings, but for the most part mixology bars will join the ranks of tiki bars; few and far between. Some of the establishments now offering mixology drinks will survive by simply changing their offerings (see CLASSIC COCKTAILS). These are the places that tend to be high-end restaurants whose main thrust is food. But those establishments that are all-in for mixology, those that have adopted all of the fashionable attributes of the trend, will soon begin to look quaint and dated—When it's done, it's done.

43

## How to determine if you're in a Mixology Bar:

- The bartender wears suspenders and/or an old time newspaper boy cap.
- The bartender precisely measures every primary ingredient.
- The bartender tastes every drink he makes with a straw.
- The bartender is igniting citrus peel over the drinks.
- The bartender is spanking his mint.
- The bar is over-staffed.
- There are jars containing what appears to be Victorian science experiments on the back-bar.
- There is no soda gun.
- The barroom has the look and feel of a movie set.
- There's a gratuitous number of squirt bottles lined up in the bartender's work station.
- The bar and everything in it is brand new and squeaky clean.
- The bartender shakes his up drinks in a very violent manner, which over-dilutes the booze and produces ice chips, which requires him to double strain them.
- You sat down over twenty minutes ago, ordered your drink over ten minutes ago and you still don't have a drink in your hand.
- Most customers are ordering their drinks from a drink menu.
- There's a guy sawing a block of ice to make ice cubes.
- The bartender uses expressions like, *flavor profile* and *driven* (as in, *This drink has a very citrus driven flavor profile*).
- You suspect that you're being duped.
- You have the nagging feeling that all of this extravagance will soon collapse of its own dead weight.

If your answer is *Yes* to one or two of the above, then you're just in a bar that's trying to cash-in on current trends. If it's *Yes* to three or four, then you're in a high-end restaurant bar. If it's *Yes* to five or more, then you're definitely in a mixology bar.

NOTE: The difference between a mixologist (or cocktologist) and a bartender is that the former view themselves as liquid chefs, the latter view themselves as legal drug dealers.

# Classic Cocktails

**T**HE OPPOSITE OF MIXOLOGY DRINKS are Classic Cocktails. These are as they sound; drinks that have stood the test of time. Mixology drinks, even those that were invented 100 years ago, have not stood the test of time, which is why mixologists say they are reviving old recipes. Another way to view it is that they are reviving the dead who probably died for good reason.

People with more money than they knew what to do with were the ones for whom these drinks were originally invented. Demanding something new and different to out do their contemporaries, they drank any motley concoction, so long as it was complicated and expensive.

One thing I've learned as a bartender is that you can mix any combination of liquors and it will be drinkable, perhaps not good, but you can drink it. Even a *Gorilla Tit*, a drink sometimes made by bartenders at the end of a busy shift, by combining the last few drops of booze left in each empty bottle, is surprisingly drinkable. It isn't good, but it's not as bad as one would guess. So I propose, for the sake of brevity, that all drinks found on a drink menu in a mixology bar henceforth be referred to as *Gorilla Tits*. So that would leave one the choice between a Gorilla Tit or a Classic Cocktail. You decide.

# What the Regulars Order

IDEALLY, YOU SHOULD ORDER drinks that you enjoy. However, you will find that bartenders and bar regulars will often deride sweet drinks, drinks with cute names or lots of ingredients, or drinks that come out of a blender and require excessive garnishes. You may object to this, after all it's just a matter of taste and you happen to like sweet drinks. But if that's the case, when dining in a restaurant have you ever ordered a fine, aged cabernet on the rocks in a pint glass filled with coke? Or would you consider asking the bartender to put lemon juice, sugar and tincture of raspberry in that same glass of expensive cab? This is the way experienced drinkers view all those sweet, creamy, fruity drinks with four or more ingredients and festooned with gratuitous garnishes; it's kid stuff. If you want to order like an adult drinker, here are some tips:

•REGULAR DRINKERS ALWAYS DRINK THE SAME DRINK This is why you will hear bartenders say, "I may forget a customer's name, but I never forget his drink." Occasionally regulars will have something out of the ordinary; perhaps they have several alternate drinks, depending on their mood, or they just feel like trying something new. But an experienced drinker will rarely have more than two different types of drinks during a drinking session. It's also worth noting that regular drinkers rarely become demonstrably drunk or vomit.

•**REGULAR DRINKERS ORDER DRINKS THAT HAVE NO MORE THAN TWO PRIMARY INGREDIENTS** Example of these would be; beer, gin and tonic, Jim Beam over, martinis, manhattans, etc.

•**ORDERING NEAT** If you want to try some liquor that you have never had before, order it neat with a water back and alternate between sips of booze and water. This way you will be able to taste it and decide if it's something you like. Experienced drinkers rarely shoot booze, they sip it. If you shoot it that usually means you don't like the taste of booze; it is an acquired taste and regular drinkers have acquired the taste for booze. Or it means you're in a hurry—regulars are rarely in a hurry, they have all the time they need and if they don't, they make time.

The use of sophisticated technology by unsophisticated people.

# The Hopster's Choice!

## GUZZEL & BURP
### BRAND BEER

**An Old World Tradition, brewed for American taste.**

Is it truly the nectar
of the gods, or just
the urine of yeast?
You decide.

Answer: Both are
correct, yeast are
the gods.

Just Guzzle it,
then Burp; it's
that easy!

Also try our dark
beer; Guzzle &
Belch or our ale;
Guzzle and Piss on
Yourself.

**Coming soon; Cat Piss Bock**

# Beer Snobbery

**T**HE MICROBREW REVOLUTION happened several decades ago, but the beer snobs have only arrived in the last decade. Effete decadents order flights of beer, swirl and sniff their glasses and make knowledgeable comments about the beer's attributes to their friends or someone sitting nearby. They stop short of spitting the beer out after swirling it over their palate, though that will likely enter the picture soon.

Added to their effete rituals, beer snobs tend to favor ales that are over hopped to the point of skunkyness and the microbreweries are happy to accommodate them. There are exceptions, but very few of these microbreweries are able to brew a decent lager or pilsner. Perhaps this is because they don't want to invest the time and expense to lager beer or because lagers are more temperamental to brew than ales. Another reason is that these breweries and their customers associate lagers with mass produced beers of the American style that took hold after prohibition and were greatly reduced in quality after the Second World War.

I'm an addict, not a connoisseur, so I prefer undelicious beer, light in body and flavor. And cold, very cold. Ales almost always have a strong flavor, which gets in the way of my drinking enjoyment. I also find that ales leave me with a worse hangover than lagers or pilsners. I like German beer the best... all of those so-and-so bergers or such-and-such steiners. The Japanese also make some great undelicious beer.

Of course there's a time and place for everything. When I drink in the afternoon I usually drink stout or porter. I tend to drink ale when eating sandwiches, salads or pizza, but on those occasions I usually have just one. When I'm out drinking recreationally I never have just one. As a friend of mine in L.A. used to say, "The hardest thing in the world to drink is one beer."

## A Brief History of Beer Snobbery

In the late sixties I was a teenager living in the South Bay area of L.A. County. At the time, my friends and I considered Michelob to be the best beer available; we drank it on special occasions only. I was drafted in 1969 and when I was released two years later I returned to L.A. to attend classes at El Camino J.C. Eventually I moved from the neighborhood where I grew up, in North Torrance, to an apartment in Manhattan Beach. Maybe it was the two years away, maybe it was college, maybe it was my new upscale neighborhood, but I soon discovered imported beer. Friends were drinking it and there was a liquor store near my apartment that boasted over one hundred different bottles of imported beer. During this same period friends took me to The Oar House in Venice Beach where I was introduced to Anchor Steam Beer.

Soon I was trying all different types of beer. Usually only one per drinking session, before switching back to the more affordable American style lagers. After three years I was forced by the veteran's advisor to move on to a four year school or forfeit my remaining GI Bill education benefits. I chose Hayward State, which is how I ended up in the Bay Area.

While in college I developed a taste for ale. At the time there were only two American examples of which I was aware: Rainier Ale (The Green Death) and Ballantine Ale, but others would soon follow. Sometime in the 80s a brew pub opened in Hayward. I was living in San Francisco by then, so I never went, but I was aware of it. Several microbreweries and brew pubs followed and, inspired by the success of Anchor, they all began by brewing ale (Anchor itself introduced Anchor Liberty Ale in 1976).

After years of a small range of flavor offered by brewers, Americans were eager to try anything new. By the 90s, due to growing demand, there were hundreds of micro-breweries spread across the U.S., each one trying to out do the next with a new take on ale, wheat beer, stout, porter, etc. With a growing field of competitors, breweries vied for shelf space in liquor stores or refrigerator/tap space in bars. This competition led to some good beer and to a lot of bad beer, as the micro-brewers tried every combination under the sun in an attempt to distance themselves from their rivals.

The growing interest in microbrews drew in people who weren't beer drinkers. This new group brought with them their interest in "the finer things," along with a distain for anything blue collar, a prejudice probably acquired from their parents. This last group to join the ranks of beer drinkers are the beer snobs. Looking down on any beer that doesn't have the proper pedigree, they project elitism, something not previously associated with beer drinkers. Beer has been the working man's drink since the time of the Ancient Babylonians and Egyptians.

Unlike mixology, microbreweries and the beer snobbery they engender are showing no signs of imminent collapse. However, those of us who find this snobbishness annoying, can take comfort in the likelihood that eventually the beer snobs will mature and come to the same conclusion beer drinkers the world over already have (including myself)… for recreational drinking, lagers are the way to go.

What cocktail waitresses talk about:

# Tipping

**T**HE WORD *TIPS*, **I'VE BEEN TOLD**, is an acronym for *To Insure Prompt Service*. Whether that's true or not, that's what your tips do for you.

•**WHY?** Tipping is customary in the United States in many service industries. Tips are an important component of the incomes of bellhops, taxi drivers, beauticians, and hotel maids (among others), but it is waiters/waitresses and bartenders for whom tips account for well over half of their income.

Tipping arose as an incentive for efficiency, and in the bar/restaurant industry, efficiency is in high demand. Because of the dynamics created by tipping, bartending in the U.S. is essentially piece work; the more pieces of work you complete during your shift, the more money you make. Consequently, bartenders are compelled to work very efficiently, which is what both customers and bar management desire.

Wages for bar and restaurant employees are low to very low, depending on where they work. Besides the low wages, bartenders generally do not receive benefits such as paid vacations, health care (though this is changing), or even sick pay—missing a shift for any reason, including illness, without getting someone to cover your shift, is grounds for dismissal.

Besides low wages and few benefits, bar management estimates tips based on the ring and deducts it from the bartender's wages. At the end of the year she pays taxes on wages and estimated tips. This being the case, when a bartender is stiffed or tipped below the percentage at which tips are estimated, she pays taxes on money that she didn't receive.

For these reasons, bartenders depend heavily on tips. If not for tips, most bartenders working today would be forced to leave the profession for financial reasons. Those that couldn't find alternative employment and remained bartenders would find themselves living in greatly reduced circumstances.

Those drawn to the void left by the departed would be the same people drawn to other low-paying jobs. I have no doubt that they could perform all the tasks necessary to make a drink and the other incidental tasks required of the job, but the quality of service would suffer and the social aspect across the bar would disappear.

For a possible illustration of what such bars would be like look to England, where virtually all pubs are owned by a corporation, usually a large brewery, and the staff is low paid and not tipped. I've worked with both an Irish and an English bartender; both told me that bartending isn't a job you want in their home countries. The Irish bartender told me that he was shocked at the end of his first shift in an American bar when he was given his share of the tips, "I didn't know that a bartender could make so much money." NOTE: Englishmen, who live where tipping isn't customary, pay more for their drinks at the local pub than Americans pay at their neighborhood bar. Numerous times a visitor from England has commented to me about how cheap it is to drink in the U.S.

Another thing to consider is that the bar staff in large U.S. cities are comprised of a fair percentage of employees with college educations, generally with degrees in the humanities, who are waiting for their big break. Even among those with no college experience, many have outside interests in the arts. Over the years I have worked with many artists, writers, musicians, etc. In fact, one of them is an editor of this book.

And U.S. bars are generally staffed with persons who reflect the general age and income of the customers they serve. They also tend to come from the community they serve and often attend social events with the regulars. If tipping were to disappear that would change. Bartenders would no longer be part of the community they serve and would have little in common with their customers who would rarely see them, except at work.

The bottom line is: If you can't afford to tip, you can't afford to drink in a bar. If you don't like it, I recommend that you to go to the Best Happy Hour in Town, your local liquor store, where the drinks are cheap and you don't have to tip. But if you crave the social aspect found in bars, then learn how to tip, both for the bartender's benefit and your own.

•**HOW MUCH?** This is the big question for people who are unfamiliar with the practice. The old rule of thumb is to leave a dollar per drink. But with rising prices that rule is becoming outdated, and it never did work in high end bars and restaurants or with top shelf brands. If you go by percentages, an average tip is 15-18%. A low tip is 10%. 20% or more is a high tip.

The easiest way to figure your tip, and one which will work in any situation for the foreseeable future, is to leave a one dollar tip for every five dollars. For instance, if your bill is fifteen dollars, leave a three dollar tip. There are bound to be fractions, especially when ordering rounds, so just round up or down depending on what you feel is right under the circumstances.

If you're leaving a stingy tip then you might as well be stiffing, particularly if you're drinking call or top-shelf booze. From the bartender's perspective, if you're drinking good booze and leaving a small tip, you're using money that should be used for tipping to buy yourself better booze.

If you're ordering more than one drink you can get away with a bit less per drink. Another consideration is the complexity of the drinks you order. If you're ordering highballs, booze neat, or beer, you can get away with a little less on average per drink, especially if you're ordering multiples of the same drink: Making five gin-and-tonics requires little more time and effort than making one.

But if you're ordering drinks that call for three or more ingredients, Bloody Marys and coffee drinks, etc., or up drinks, especially those that call for sugared rims or other such flourishes, then you should round up, especially if everyone in your group orders something different. Also note that bartenders expect a larger tip from people who use credit cards because they involve extra time and effort.

•**WHO SHOULD BE TIPPED?** You should tip anyone who makes or serves you a drink. Those bussing tables or restocking the bar (bar-backs) get tipped out by the bartenders and waiters, so it isn't necessary to tip them. Occasionally bar-backs, unless they are prohibited from this by management, will make drinks when the bartender is slammed. Under these circumstances, they should be tipped just like a bartender.

Some people seem to think that they have to tip waitresses, who are transporting drinks, but that they don't need to tip bartenders because they're just standing there. These are the jokers who typically sit at a table, but go to the bar for their drinks. These people are getting on the bad side of both the waitress, whose table space they're taking up, and the bartender who they're stiffing. **BOTTOM LINE:** If you're drinking in a bar you should be tipping someone. **NOTE:** Ideally, if you're sitting in the waitress' section you should be tipping her, whether you are getting your drinks from her or directly from the bartender. You are, by sitting in her section, taking up the limited space she has in which to make her nightly income. When you get up to go, you should leave her something for the use of her space.

•**WHO SHOULD TIP?** Anyone who drinks in a bar: Friends of the owner (friends of the owner who don't tip are resented by the bar staff), friends of the bartender's (then he'll probably buy you a drink), persons who receive a free drink (even for their birthday), women (no matter how pretty), men (no matter how macho), persons who feel they work harder for their money than bartenders (come stand in my shoes for ten minutes in the middle of a slammed Saturday night shift) and persons who can't afford to tip (see **WHY?** above).

•**WHEN?** My advice is to tip after each round of drinks. Some people feel that they should tip in one big chunk when they are ready to go. If you're a regular and the bartender knows you, this is okay. But if the bartender isn't familiar with you, then you should definitely tip after every round. If you don't the bartender will assume you're a stiff and you'll find it increasingly difficult to get a drink. Bartenders assess each customer's tipping habits and all they have to go on is the tips they see falling on the bar. If they see nothing, they have to assume there is no tip. **NOTE:** Leaving a large pile of money on the bar and using it to pay for your drinks gives the bartender no indication of what sort of a tipper you are, and in my experience people who do this tend to be cheapskates. I guess they think they've found a way to get good service; by leaving what appears to be a huge tip on the bar, then leaving tiny tips by picking up most or all of it when they're ready to go. So unless it's a bar where you drink regularly, don't pay from a pile of cash. It also gives other bar patrons the opportunity to rob you.

•**WITH WHAT?** Bills. You should avoid using coins for any transaction in a bar, unless they were part of your change.

•**WILL THE BARTENDER NOTICE I'VE LEFT HIM A TIP?** Yes, usually. Bartenders tend to pay attention to who's tipping and who isn't, even when the bar is slammed. But if you want to make sure you get credit for your tip, make your tip as obvious as possible. Try to leave your tip while the bartender is still facing you. This can be difficult if the bartender is slammed and has moved on to the next customer before you can accomplish this. If you've just made a trip to the bar for a drink and have an empty glass or bottle in your hand, leave your tip under it. When the bartender returns to bus your glass, the tip will be there, and the glass can help jog the bartender's memory as to who left it, particularly if you're drinking the same drink each round. This will also prevent your tip from getting knocked off the bar or mixed up with someone else's tip or change.

By far the best way to insure that the bartender is aware of your tip is to wave off the change, or to simply walk away without collecting it when the bartender returns from the register. Of course, this doesn't work if you're paying with a bill that's far larger than your payment.

•**WILL THE BARTENDER GET HER TIP AFTER A SHIFT CHANGE?** Usually. The bartender taking over will generally scan the bar for tips from the previous shift and give them to her before she leaves. If she's already gone he'll put it in the drop with her name on it. But sometimes, if the bar is busy during a shift change, this will be difficult to determine. If you want to make sure she gets your tip you can hand it to her when she's about to go off shift.

•**When a tip is implied in your payment** If your payment is in the form of two or more bills and one or more of them is left unbroken by the exchange, the bartender will interpret the remainder as a tip. For instance, your order comes to $4.50. If you give the bartender $5.00, you will get fifty-cents in change. If you give the bartender $6.00, you will get nothing in change. Why? Because there's no reason to add the extra dollar to your payment unless it's a tip; five covers the transaction. If you are involved in the above transaction and want to give the bartender a one-dollar tip, then give her $5.00 to cover your order and when you receive the fifty cents change, pick it up and put the dollar in its place.

The only time this rule doesn't hold is when the extra amount is far greater than a good tip. For instance, your order comes to $10 and all you have is a ten and a five, so you give the bartender both bills. Most bartender's will recognize that you want five singles so that you can leave a proper tip, because a 50% tip is out of the norm. However, my advice would be to ask for singles to avoid any possible confusion, particularly near the end of the month when rent's due.

•**Fluffing the change** Often the size of an expected tip is inferred by your change. Your order comes to $4.50, you pay with a ten and get five ones and two quarters in change. This is a hint: the bartender is saying that 50 cents isn't going to cut it as a tip. You don't have to leave more, but if you don't, your next round may take awhile.

•**Don't fluff my change** The bill comes to five dollars and the customer gives the bartender a ten dollar bill and a one dollar bill; most bartenders will recognize that the dollar is his tip and the customer wants a fiver in change rather than a fist full of ones.

•**Free drinks** You should always tip for a free drink, at least as

63

much as you would have tipped had you paid for the drink; ideally, you should tip more.

•**RESTAURANT BARS** When having a drink at the bar in a restaurant while waiting for a table, always leave a tip at the bar before being seated at your table, otherwise the bartender will end up getting fifteen cents on the dollar of the tip you intend for him.

•**WHEN IT'S UNNECESSARY TO TIP** Cigarettes, matches and water, snacks/bar kibble, when provided to you by the bartender, don't require a tip. However, if you're drinking a lot of water, asking for one glass after another, you should consider tipping.

•**NURSING DRINKS** Even if you tip well and otherwise behave yourself you can run afoul of your bartender if you sit there and nurse one drink all night long. This is especially true on a busy night. The bartender only has so much time and space to make his living each night. If you're taking up valuable space at the bar, but not buying more than one drink an hour, the bartender will become increasingly annoyed by your presence.

•**WHAT TIPS WON'T GET YOU** A tip won't buy you friendship or get you a date with a bartender, it won't necessarily get you extra alcohol or free drinks, and it doesn't give you the right to act like a fool. A bartender may give you a free drink if you're a good tipper, but don't expect it. You can tip 100%, but if you're arrogant, obnoxious, or annoying, you won't get anything extra. If you push it too far, you'll be cut off and/or bounced. Tipping insures prompt service and will usually make your interactions with the bartender more pleasant. Everything else must be earned.

•**A CREDIT CARD MYSTERY** I've noticed over the past few years that some credit card customers will leave perplexing tips, such as $2.08. Why they do this I'm not sure. Perhaps they use the calculator on their smart phone to calculate exactly 12%, or maybe it's some form of code they use to remind themselves of where they spent the money. It's also possible that they do it just to annoy the bartender. What ever the reason, when I'm confronted by such a tip I simply adjust it to an even amount.

•ONE ADDITIONAL REASON TO TIP Since bars are social meeting places and they are presided over by the bartender, it behooves you to be on his good side. A bartender can help or hinder your social interactions while in his domain. For instance, it won't facilitate your efforts to impress the woman sitting next to you if the bartender calls attention to your cheapness.

Or, if you are that woman and you've been stiffing the bartender, he isn't likely to intercede when the cheapskate seated next to you begins to tell you long-winded stories about how fast he drives his Corvette.

Besides this, in most bars you will encounter regulars who view the bar as their living room and the bartender as *their* bartender. All regulars tip; if they didn't they wouldn't be regulars, they would be annoying customers. And these regulars don't like it when they see a stranger stiff their bartender. If they do, believe me, your stock will drop.

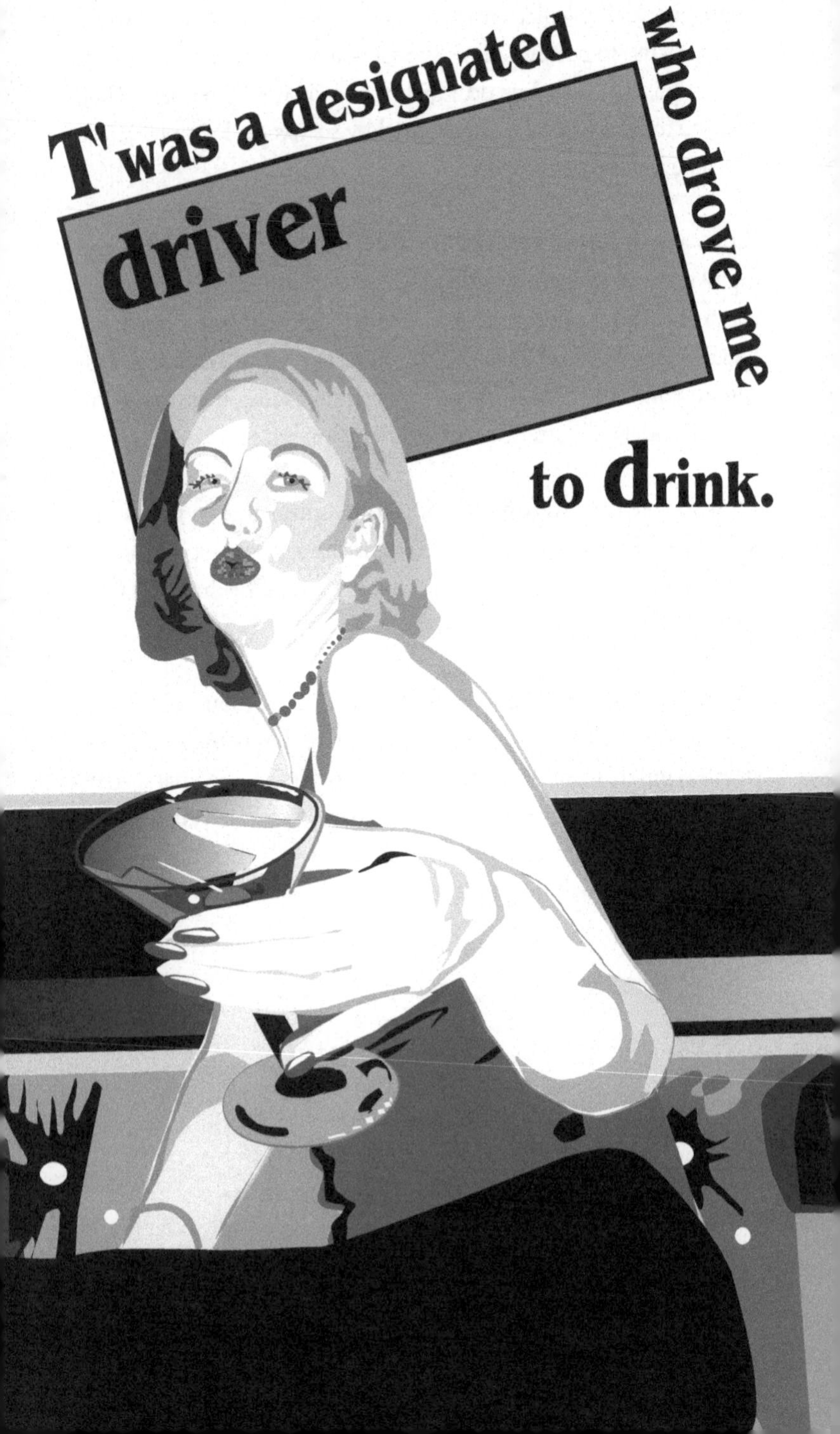
T'was a designated
driver
who drove me
to drink.

# The Product

**S**IT IN A BAR LONG ENOUGH and you will hear numerous beliefs concerning the attributes of alcohol. They run the gamut from aesthetics to health to the types of highs you get from different beverages. I can make no claims as to the scientific validity of any of my beliefs, but as a bartender for over a quarter century and a drinker for close to half a century, I am entitled to my opinion. With that disclaimer firmly established, what follows is a brief list of my opinions.

• **TASTE** Sometimes you will have a drink and it won't taste the way you expect it to taste. Perhaps it's a favorite beverage you've had many times before, but this time it doesn't taste quite right. You suspect the bartender has dishonestly slipped you well booze in place of the more expensive call liquor you paid for. Sometimes this is the case, but it's far more likely that one of the following has happened:

**1)** You've been drinking or eating something else before ordering the current drink or you're coming down with a cold; in either case your sense of taste may be affected.

**2)** The bartender has mistakenly served you the wrong booze. Sometimes this is because the bartender has misunderstood you or has gotten confused (bartenders often have more than one thing on their minds). Sometimes, in the case of well booze, the bottles in the speed well have inadvertently been switched and the bartender has poured the wrong booze (The bottles in the well are always kept in the same order so the bartender doesn't have to look each time he reaches for one. If the bottles become mixed up it's as if the keys on your keyboard were rearranged).

**3)** Your drink has been contaminated; in the case of vodka martinis it doesn't take much. If the bartender hasn't bothered to rinse out his mixing vessel the residue from the last drink could alter the taste of your martini. Or if he has recently opened a new bottle of vodka and put a pour spout on it that hasn't been rinsed out, whatever booze that spout was previously on will contaminate the taste of your drink.

•**APPEARANCES** Sometimes a drink will look different than you expect it to look. This can be caused by the lighting in the bar or by the type of glassware used by the bar.

•**NO-HANGOVER BOOZE** There is no such thing. It's an advertising ploy used by certain vodka makers and is based on a partial truth: It has been found that trace substances in the amber-colored liquors can cause health problems over the long run, in the short run they can add to your hangover misery. When vodka makers claim they've removed all the impurities, rendering their product hangover-free, what they fail to mention is that alcohol itself is an impurity, so far as your body is concerned, and it makes up 40% of their product. The only sure way to avoid a hangover is abstinence. Drink enough of any alcoholic beverage and you will get a hangover.

•**PEOPLE WHO DON'T GET HANGOVERS** There is scientific evidence that about 20% of people don't get hangovers, but for the other 80% of us, anyone who drinks enough to get drunk will get a hangover. Perhaps not every time, but more often than not. Some drinkers who claim they never get hangovers are probably chronic alcoholics. They drink to the same degree of drunkenness everyday and every morning they wake up feeling the same, so they say they don't get hangovers. If you woke up, feeling the way they feel when they wake up, you'd call it a hangover.

•**DRINKING WATER TO AVOID A HANGOVER** Alcohol is a diuretic. Hangovers are due, in part, to dehydration. The theory is to counteract this by drinking large quantities of water. It probably also helps by cutting down on the amount of alcohol you drink during the course of an evening, because it takes time to drink water that might otherwise be spent drinking alcohol.

•**DRINKING UP THE LADDER** There's a popular belief that you will avoid getting sick if you drink up, rather than down the ladder. What this means is that if you've been drinking wine and want to change beverages, you should choose distilled spirits, not beer for your next drink. I don't know if this works, but I see no reason it should. Casting further doubt on the validity of this belief is the opposing view that you should drink down rather than up the ladder.

Personally, I break this rule every time I eat out in a restaurant. I start with a martini before dinner, drink wine with my dinner, have a shot of bourbon or rye after dinner and when my dinner has settled, I switch to beer. I have never vomited due to drinking like this. If drinking causes you to vomit, it's because you've had too much.

•**DRINKING ON AN EMPTY STOMACH** The reason people warn you against this is because food in your stomach slows your absorption of alcohol, so you don't get drunk as quickly. Of course there is the opposing view point: You get more bang for the buck drinking on an empty stomach.

•**Drinking beer on a full stomach** From personal experience I can attest that this isn't a good idea. The reason why is that beer, when thrown on top of a large meal, particularly one containing a lot of carbohydrates, causes the contents of the stomach to swell.

•**Mixing alcoholic beverages** There is a commonly held belief that mixing alcoholic beverages causes hangovers and/or makes you sick. There could be something to this, but I doubt it. What's really going on here is inexperienced drinking. If you watch experienced drinkers, they drink the same thing all night at a very regular rate. They drink the same thing every night they go out. In this way they gauge how drunk they are getting. Experienced drinkers know how drunk they should be at any given point in the evening. If they feel they're getting ahead of themselves, they back off for a while. Offer them something different than what they've been drinking and they will tell you, "I don't change horses midstream."

Inexperienced drinkers jump from one thing to the next, sipping one, shooting another, guzzling the one after that. Mid-drink their friend orders a round of shots; they do them at once, then return to the drink in progress. First, it's a cosmopolitan, then a shot of Jaegermeister, then a Long Island Iced Tea. These people are hammered before they know what hit them. That night they throw up. The next morning they awake with a horrible hangover and blame it all on the fact that they were mixing their drinks. It wasn't the mixture, it was the quantity and the rate.

•**Hair of the dog** A time-honored hangover cure the drinking world over. The expression stems from a folk medicine belief which dates back to before the Romans. This form of health care holds that if something ails you, you need to ingest a minute quantity of the agent suspected of causing your disease. In full form the expression is, "A hair of the dog that bit you," apparently referring to a guard against rabies; ingest a hair of the dog that bit you (or place a hair in the bite wound), and you will avoid getting rabies. Drinkers using this excuse for a morning drink are entering a vicious cycle. A drink will definitely cure a hangover, but it does so by getting you drunk again. When it wears off, you will find yourself in need of another curative.

•**DIFFERENT HIGHS FROM DIFFERENT BEVERAGES** I have personally never noticed this to be the case, but many people claim to get a different high from tequila than they do from beer than they do from wine. I do notice that I get drunker and do stupider things if I drink distilled spirits along with my beer, rather than just sticking to beer. Heavier-bodied beers seem to make me feel more relaxed than light-bodied ones. But it all seems to be more or less the same feeling— drunkenness.

I have drank tequila, Jagermeister and Absinthe and never felt anything but drunk. Once, in Mexico, I drank something I was told was called *Raicilla*. I was also told by the bartender, who poured it from an unmarked bottle he kept under the bar, that it was illegal in Mexico. I woke up the next morning with a terrible hangover, but had felt nothing but drunk the night before. On the other hand, when I've smoked pot or opium, taken LSD or snorted cocaine, I've felt quite a bit different. Maybe I'm just insensitive.

•**NON-ALCOHOLIC BEER** Bars carry this product primarily for alcoholics who are on the wagon or who have quit indefinitely, but whose lives still revolve around bars. People who don't have a drinking problem will drink real beer if that's what they want to taste. People who have never been drinkers have no reason to want something that tastes vaguely like beer; they will order soda pop, water or juice. Two of the exceptions to this rule are: Pregnant women or others forced to avoid alcohol for medical reasons, and designated drivers.

•**HISTORY** Alcohol is a naturally occurring substance and has been around since before man walked the earth. I have seen nature shows in which giraffes, monkeys and other wild animals have gotten drunk by eating fermented fruit.

Mead (fermented water and honey) is probably the first alcoholic beverage. It's likely that mead occurred naturally prior to man's existence. How this could be is documented in Homer's *The Odyssey*. All that's required to make Mead is honey, water and yeast. In The Odyssey, Odysseus comes across a hollow honey tree that had been knocked down in a storm and filled with rain water. Wild yeast fell into the honey-water mixture and basic mead was the result.

•**HICCUPS** The bartender's cure for the hiccups is lime and bitters. Put a lime wedge in a rocks glass and soak it with four or five dashes of bitters (some bartenders first dip the lime into sugar). The hiccup sufferer then shoots the whole business into his mouth, chews it up and swallows it. This doesn't work every time, but it beats all of the other hiccup cures.

•**SLEEP** Alcohol can have a damaging effect on the quality of your sleep. If you don't believe this now, someday you will. It's possible that you've already experienced sleep deprivation due to alcohol and not realized it. It's easy to pass out when you're drunk, but passed out sleep isn't as refreshing as real sleep and you tend to wake up still tired.

The second type of sleep deprivation is insomnia. You may experience it either upon going to bed drunk and finding it impossible to fall asleep or, more likely, after passing out for four or five hours and then waking up in a wired state, unable to fall back to sleep. I've been told by many people (none of them doctors) that this is due to the sugars in alcoholic beverages. Alcohol is sugar that has been converted by the action of yeast. The yeast organisms eat sugar, then excrete alcohol; this process is called fermentation (that's right, alcohol is the urine of yeast). The idea is that when the alcohol wears off, the excess energy generated by the digestion of the residual sugars, in incompletely fermented or sweetened beverages, causes you to become wired. There could be something to this, but I suspect it's a little more complex than that.

•CURE FOR THE COMMON COLD Some people feel that a shot of whiskey, perhaps mixed with hot water and a little sugar, is a way to deal with a cold. While it will make you feel better, (just as some over-the-counter cold remedies that are 40% alcohol do) it has no effect on your cold other than to lower your body's defenses to the virus which is causing your problems. The best thing you can do when you come down with a cold is to lay off the sauce.

•SEX Much the same as sleep, you will eventually have problems in this area, even if up until now you've noticed no effect or even had an enhancement of sexual abilities. It will affect different people at different ages, but eventually alcohol takes its toll. Only men will be directly affected, but it certainly can't be a source of joy to a person whose sexual partner is unable to perform after imbibing too much.

However, on average, alcohol takes a greater toll on a woman's appearance than on a man's. So, though a woman who regularly drinks too much may still be able to perform sexually, she will find it increasingly difficult to attract acceptable partners.

•EATING/WEIGHT EFFECTS Alcohol is the only drug that has food value. An ounce of beer has about 13 calories. An ounce of wine has about 20 calories. And an ounce of distilled spirits has about 53 calories. If your weekly diet stays the same but you add to it several drinks, then it's possible to add several hundred calories to your diet and a weight gain could result.

However, since alcohol contains calories, the effect of one or more drinks is often to suppress your appetite. If the calories you consume, in the form of alcohol, are offset by an equal number of calories lost by not eating, you may experience no weight gain. If you expend extra calories due to supplementary activities caused by drinking, then you could actually lose weight. Conversely, if drinking causes you to become more sedentary you may gain weight even though you are consuming the same number of calories.

If drinking becomes a problem and calories from alcohol supplant much of your caloric intake from other sources, then you will not only lose weight but your body will begin to deteriorate. The reason for this is that the calories found in alcohol are devoid of nutritional value and your body will be forced to cannibalize bones and internal organs for nutrients necessary for metabolism. The fact that alcohol is a diuretic is another problem. Many alcoholics suffer from dehydration, which adds to weight loss and has serious health consequences.

•HEALTH PROBLEMS In addition to those mentioned above, there is a host of health problems related to alcohol. As I have no medical training, I can only point out a few of the obvious ones. I'm sure a doctor could add to this list:
•CIRRHOSIS OF THE LIVER
•INCREASED RISK OF CANCER
•HEART PROBLEMS
•GENERAL LOWERING OF PERSONAL HYGIENE STANDARDS leading to other health problems.
•CUTS, BRUISES, BROKEN BONES, LOSS OF TEETH
•THE D.T.'S / Mental disorientation.
•DEPRESSION
•ACCIDENTAL DEATH due to falls, traffic accidents, boating accidents, house fires, alcohol poisoning, extreme dissipation, exposure to the elements, etc.
•LOSS OF PRODUCTIVITY You will miss more work, clean your house less, make payments of bills in a less timely fashion, pay less atten-

tion to your personal appearance, have less money to spend on other interests in your life, have less other interests in your life, fail in your social relationships more often, spend more time in jail and/or court, be more likely to have your driver's license suspended or revoked, pay more for car insurance, lose more jobs, spend more on doctor bills and be more likely to default on bank loans if you allow alcohol to run your life.

For more graphic information on this subject you need look no further than city streets; huddled there you will find legions of people who went too far in their love for alcohol.

## ON THE OTHER HAND...

•**HEALTH BENEFITS** A few drinks a day can have a beneficial effect on your health. Lower blood pressure and lower stress levels are two that come to mind. There is some evidence that alcohol in moderation can lower cholesterol levels. Whatever the claims or evidence the key is moderation, which means one to three drinks per day, depending on the gender and size of the individual. More than that and the benefits are outweighed by the negative effects.

•**RECREATION** While more than three drinks can be harmful there is such a thing as being too health-conscious. Life is should be enjoyed; a long, dull life isn't something I feel is worth pursuing. Occasionally, getting drunk can be worth the increased health risk just for the enjoyment. Climbing mountains, skiing, travel and sex can be health threats too, but people choose to indulge in these activities because they weigh the health threat against the amount of enjoyment derived. The same can be said for occasionally over-indulging in your favorite beverage.

•**SOCIAL ACTIVITIES** Most interaction can be enhanced and revved up by the introduction of alcohol. People become more animated under the influence of alcohol and this can add excitement to any social situation. Dancing is more fun if you're a bit looped, as are long conversations in a bar with friends, acquaintances and strangers. Parties are fueled by alcohol. I have noticed over the years that when the alcohol runs out, especially alcohol in the form of beer, the party dies.

•**FOOD** One of the reasons alcohol is so prominent in western culture is that it goes well with food, and is itself a food product. A martini before dinner builds anticipation for the coming meal. Wine with dinner enhances the flavor of the food and aids digestion. An after-dinner drink such as bourbon, scotch or brandy also aids digestion and is very relaxing. The only other drugs that play a part in a good meal are tobacco and coffee, but their roles are minor in comparison. Oh yeah, and pot, which is not so much an enhancement to a good meal as it is an agent used to make any food product seem appealing in large quantities.

•**RESTORATIVE POWERS** There's nothing like a beer after work. It relaxes you as it quenches your thirst, soothes aching muscles and brightens your outlook on life.

•**PAIN KILLER** Whether it's an aching back or an aching heart, alcohol can help. While I wouldn't recommend it for sufferers of mental illness or long term problems, its ability to brighten your outlook on life in the short term can help you to overcome the minor aches, pains and depressions of life.

•**CONVERSATION** One of the truly positive experiences associated with alcohol is its effect on conversation. What would otherwise be a minor disagreement becomes a full-fledged argument. A subject, which had seemed dull or off limits in polite society, now commands enthusiastic attention. What began as a boring evening has turned into an exciting one, thanks to that old demon alcohol.

•**IDEAS** Many good ideas come with the help of a little alcohol, sometimes while talking with someone, other times while just sitting alone, quietly drinking in a bar. The relaxing and uninhibiting effects of this drug allows ideas, that would otherwise be repressed, to float gently to the surface.

•**BONDING** People who drink together form bonds more readily. This is because when people drink they exhibit parts of their personalities that they would otherwise hide. If you know them in their sober state, this additional information about them can help to cement a relationship. But if drunk is the only way you encounter them the relationship probably won't be a very sound one.

•**JOINT PROJECTS** Just as with personal relationships, projects can benefit by occasional meetings in bars. People loosen up; alcohol brings them together and levels the social strata. The boss gets drunk when she drinks, just like everybody else. An underling feels free to voice doubts about some aspect of the project. People become jovial, bonds among team members are strengthened. This goes for groups of artists as well as for groups of engineers.

•**MEETING PEOPLE** Because alcohol lowers inhibitions, it's great for meeting people. Sitting in a bar you are more likely to strike up a conversation with a stranger and the stranger is more likely to respond positively when you do. Shy people have newfound social skills and the already socially adept don't know where to turn next for a new conversation with a new face.

•**PROBLEM SOLVING** There is no intractable national or world problem that can't be solved in a 45 minute session by three drunks at the end of the bar. Having noticed this (and occasionally been one of those three drunks) I propose that the United States congress be reconfigured into a bar. Having proposed this I would like to be considered for the post of Congressional Bartender.

•**AMOUR** If you're looking for physically intimate contact, alcohol is a proven catalyst. It's no guarantee, but your chances improve when alcohol enters the picture. Someone who was mildly attractive to you earlier in the evening may begin to look much better after a few drinks. As a friend of mine once bragged, "I've never been to bed with an ugly woman, but I've woken up with dozens of them—I drink 'em pretty." Luckily, alcohol has the same effect on women.

The danger here, as we all know, is waking up with someone you'd rather not wake up with. It can be an awkward moment upon awakening to find yourself in a strange bed in a strange part of town with someone whose name you can't recall, the sun streaming through the window and no shades in your pocket. This can be more than embarrassing or humiliating, it can be dangerous. The best advice is not to get so drunk that you make bad decisions. Of course, advice is much easier to give than to receive.

The fashion pendulum
has come to a stop...

from now on
everything will be
in fashion—forever.

# Who's in Charge Here?

**O**NE THING EVERY BARTENDER KNOWS is that he must remain in charge of the bar at all times. If you let an unruly, arrogant, violent or drunk person take charge for even a moment, you're asking for trouble. If you let it happen on a regular basis, you're out of a job. This is one of the hardest parts of bartending; any fool can pour gin into a glass and hand it to a drunk. It takes a little more intelligence to keep that drunk happy while you're telling him he's had too much and that you won't serve him anymore.

For this reason bartenders will let you know when you've stepped over the line. All bartenders realize that in a bar, what would be considered aberrant behavior elsewhere, is to be expected. To what degree it is tolerated depends on the parameters of the particular bar and bartender. However, there are some guidelines that apply in pretty much every bar:

•**B**RINGING YOUR OWN DRINKS INTO/OUT OF A BAR Unless you're in New Orleans, Savannah, or another place where to-go cups are legal, don't do this. Bartenders will stop patrons from taking their drinks out of their bar because it is illegal. Bartenders will stop patrons bringing their own drinks into their bar because they're in the business of selling booze. Open containers found in the bar are viewed as a form of theft, so they are confiscated and poured out.

An exception to this no in or out rule is made for people who bring in an unopened bottle of wine or champagne and ask the bartender's permission to do so. This is usually allowed, with a corkage fee charged for each bottle opened. If it's a large party with a single bottle, the bartender will often figure it's worth the goodwill to waive the corkage fee, as they will polish the bottle off quickly, then start buying their drinks from the bar. However, once the bottle is opened, it can't be removed from the barroom.

The bottom line is that a bar is a place of business and bartenders are working to make a living. You wouldn't take a picnic lunch into a restaurant; don't bring your own drinks into a bar.

•**EXCESSIVE DRINKING** Drunks can make the job of bartending a pain in the ass. People who order strange concoctions made from several liquors and shoot them between guzzling large quantities of simpler beverages, in a silly attempt to get as drunk as possible in the shortest amount of time, don't impress bartenders, except with the fact that they're inexperienced drinkers.

Bars are places where alcohol is consumed, so bartenders expect people to get drunk. However, a point is reached where a customer becomes too drunk to be served. Beyond this point the customer will become a potential danger to all involved. At the very least he will become a source of annoyance to those around him. At this point there's no choice but to cut him off.

•**NOT ENOUGH BOOZE** Customers will occasionally return a drink because there isn't enough booze in it. These are usually people who are drinking highballs (for some reason those drinking Jack & Coke are the biggest offenders). Sometimes it's people who ordered their drink tall. It's almost always people who have been drinking a lot. I never give these jokers extra booze, I simply explain to them how they should order in the future if they want to taste the booze; with a splash of mixer or neat (straight).

•**BUYING FRIENDS DRINKS WHEN THEY DON'T WANT/NEED ONE** Often customers will offer to buy a friend a drink. This is part of drinking in a bar. However, bartenders can be expected to refuse this request in either of two scenarios: The friend in question is too drunk, or the friend in question declines the offer.

Occasionally the customer offering to buy the drink will then demand that the bartender serve the drink anyway. The customer is wrong. The bartender is in a better position to judge the situation. If the friend being offered the drink feels he or she is too drunk for another drink then it's not in the bartender's best interest to serve the drink (unless, of course, he or she likes cleaning up vomit). The same is true if the friend is obviously too drunk to handle another drink. Customers who become belligerent due to the bartender's refusal to serve their friend an additional drink are asking to be cut off themselves.

•**BUYING DRINKS FOR A PERSON WHO HAS BEEN CUT OFF** This is similar to the situation noted above. The way it usually transpires is a customer will be cut off at the bar for any of several reasons. After a brief argument with the bartender, the customer wanders away. A moment later, another customer comes up to the bar and orders the same drink that the first customer was denied. To the bartender it is obvious what's going on; he's being played for a chump.

•**BUYING THE BARTENDER A DRINK** Nothing wrong with this, if the bartender agrees. But personally I have never let a customer buy me a drink. The reason is that I don't want the customer to have a say in how drunk I get. I can drink for free while I work, but I have to stay sober... it's a razor's edge. I've known bartenders who keep a vodka bottle filled with water under the bar and when they encounter such a person they serve themselves a shot from it and pocket the money they charge. But I don't like being forced to lie. So when a customer, usually drunk and always a guy, insists on buying me a drink, I show him that I already have one going and tell him that I drink for free. This usually ends the conversation. But if it doesn't satisfy the customer, that's too bad. He drinks at my pleasure, not the other way around.

•**DOUBLES, LINING UP DRINKS** I prefer not to serve doubles or to line up drinks because it's harder to control how drunk the customer is becoming. If it's a person I'm familiar with I don't mind, because I know their drinking habits. If it's a large person I'm not concerned, because they can absorb a lot of booze. But I watch those customers unknown to me and of average size who order doubles or line up drinks. At the first sign that they're going over the deep end I cut them off.

Something to keep in mind is you generally don't get a bulk discount on booze; unless otherwise specified, a double costs twice as much as a single. The only thing you save when you order doubles is time.

•**EXCESSIVE, SUCCESSIVE SHOTS** Occasionally a person of average size will order a shot, only to order a second one moments after shooting the first. I always serve it. However, if they order a third shot less than twenty minutes after the second, I always decline their request. I know the first one is just hitting him and that the second is on its way. I want to know how number two hits him before I serve him number three.

•**GIVING A DRUNK A FREE DRINK** This doesn't save them money, they simply drink one more than planned. This being the case, if someone I'm serving seems to be near or at the tipping point, even if they're otherwise due a free drink, I don't give them one.

•CUTTING OFF DRUNKS This is a sticky wicket. To soften the blow I offer them something else, such as coffee or water and tell them they are welcome to return on another occasion. Complicating the situation is the fact that it's not always obvious that a customer is drunk. Many drunks are able to feign sobriety long enough to order a drink. Often I've served a seemingly sober person only to see him staggering around moments later. This usually happens with a customer who has just arrived from another bar where he has gotten tanked up and has subsequently been cut off. These are usually customers I'm not familiar with; I know the tells of the regulars. But with strangers, especially if they're good at hiding their inebriation, I usually have to serve them a drink before I can tell if they've had too much. Bartenders help each other out by notifying each other when they realize they've served a drunk or when a customer they've had trouble with in the past enters the bar.

In other cases it's much easier to tell. One thing that's a dead giveaway is a customer with her head on the bar. It not only looks bad to have people passed out on the bar, but it becomes a safety problem as well. It also presents a dilemma if it's near the end of the night, because you have to get rid of the customer before closing, but your options for doing so are few. No cab driver wants to pick up a comatose person because that person then becomes his problem. You can't just throw them out on the street for both ethical and legal reasons. The usual method of dealing with customers whose heads are on the bar is to rouse them and get them moving toward the door as soon as possible.

Another dead giveaway of a drunk is that he takes forever to extract his money from his wallet; fumbling with bills, counting and re-counting the contents of his wallet, then looking around in a confused manner as if to say, "I thought I had more money..."

Perhaps the most obvious signs that a customer has had too much are spilling drinks or falling off of a barstool. If a customer falls off his barstool, unless I've been suspecting him of being drunk, I assume it was an honest accident. If a customer spills his drink I replace it, if they don't seem drunk. If they spill the second drink or if they fall off their barstool a second time, I assume that they're just good at covering their drunkenness and I cut them off.

Then there are those people whom anyone can tell are drunk; they stagger in off the street, they wander around the bar talking loudly, annoying people, bumping into patrons and furniture, and generally making a nuisance of themselves. These people don't belong in a bar.

In these cases and the ones I haven't mentioned, you often find that the customer who's been cut off will want to argue the point and try to convince you that you're mistaken. Sometimes their arguments are compelling. However, I have found over the years that when I've second guessed myself in this situation, I've almost always been sorry. For years now, my rule of thumb is that once I've made the decision to cut someone off, I don't go back on it. My stock response to such arguments is, "I do make mistakes and if you feel I'm wrong you're welcome to get a second opinion at some other bar from some other bartender." And no, I never suggest a specific bar.

•THE CUSTOMER'S ALWAYS RIGHT Wrong. What you're thinking of is a department store. While on duty, the bartender's always right when it comes to matters of the bar's operation. Even when he's wrong he's right.

•DON'T TREAT THE BARTENDER AS A SERVANT Bartenders are members of the service industry. They make your drinks and serve them to you. They wipe up your spills and perform other tasks so that you can enjoy a few drinks with your friends. However, if you want to get on the bad side of a bartender, the quickest way to do so is to treat her as a servant. A couple of examples of this sort of behavior would be waving money in the air and/or yelling "Hey!" to get her attention. Another no-no is banging an empty glass on the bar.

•**NEVER WALK BEHIND THE BAR.** Not even one step.

•**LAST CALL** When last call is sounded, that's the time to order your last drink, not ten minutes later. If you wait ten minutes you probably won't get a drink. At this point the bar staff is thinking about clean-up, side work and other chores associated with closing time, not about you getting your final-final. If you do order at last call make sure you can drink it in the time remaining. Don't check your watch when the bartender tells you it's time to go. Bars exist in their own time zone, which is anywhere from five to twenty minutes ahead of the time out on the street. When a member of the bar staff tells you it's time to go, it's time to go.

•**HEY, IT'S ONLY 1 A.M., YOU HAVE TO SERVE FOR ANOTHER HOUR** No matter what state, if there's a law concerning how late a bar can serve, it's a maximum hour. No bar is forced to serve until 2 A.M. or whatever the state's law describes. For instance, in the state of California bars can be opened from 6 A.M. until 2 A.M. Few bars choose to be open for all twenty hours. They must be closed from 2 A.M. until 6 A.M., what hours they are open is up to their management.

•**DAYLIGHT SAVINGS TIME** When fall comes and the clocks are set back, can the bar serve for another hour? No. That's why time is set back at 2 A.M. when bars in most states are forced to close, otherwise it would be set back at 1 A.M.

•**DON'T TELL THE BARTENDER HOW TO DO HIS JOB** Even if you're father was a bartender or if you're from England.

# Bar Etiquette

SOME PEOPLE YOU SEE IN BARS just seem to fit in. Their manner is comfortable and they're always able to get a drink. They encounter few if any problems and they get along well with the bartender and the other customers, even if they're not regulars. Other people are always in the way of bar staff and other customers. They have trouble getting served and are often in an argument over some perceived transgression. The difference between the two groups is that the first group knows the unwritten etiquette of bars, the second group does not. What follows is my effort to change that unwritten status and while not complete, it's a start.

•GETTING THE BARTENDER'S ATTENTION This usually isn't a problem when business is moderate, but it can be when the bar is slammed. The wait probably isn't as long as you think, but when you want a drink, ten minutes can seem excessive. To help you cut down on your wait you must first see things from the bartender's perspective.

A bartender will try to serve customers in roughly the order they come to the bar. Make eye contact. This will put you on the bartender's mental waiting list. Once you've made eye contact you'll probably get a nod from the bartender; this means he's seen you and you're on his mental waiting list. At this point you should remain alert to the bartender's progress, but you can stop intently looking his way (If you continue to stare at him this will give the impression that you're impatient), instead, have your money out and visible. This tells the bartender that, at the very least, you are ready to pay and won't slow things down with a bill-by-bill inventory of your wallet, pocket or purse. Beyond that, it's been my experience that customers who have their money out also have their order ready, which is what a busy bartender wants.

•**CREDIT CARDS** Holding a credit card on the bar doesn't work as well as cash. When I scan the bar for customers during a busy shift and I see one holding cash, the other a credit card, I always go to the cash customer first. Cash transactions are simply more efficient, plus credit card customers tend to be weekend warriors who require more service.

•**GETTING SERVED** Bartenders are human and as such will be attracted to certain customers for a variety of reasons that have nothing to do with either fairness or a first-come-first-served policy: They are taller, so they stand out. They are attractive people, so they stand out. They are friends or regulars, so the bartender recognizes them. They are customers who have recently been served and left a large tip, etc. If you don't fall into any of these categories you can, by standing in close proximity to persons who do, increase your chances of being served.

For instance, you're in a very busy bar and there's a tall, attractive female waiting to get a drink. If you stand next to her you stand a good chance of being the one served right after her simply because when the bartender has completed the transaction with her, you will be standing right there. However, you must follow the other rules: Make eye contact and have your money visible. When the bartender returns to complete the transaction with her make sure that you're not chatting with friends or typing on your smart phone, because you can lose this slight advantage in an instant if the bartender returns, gives her her change, looks to you and finds that you're otherwise engaged. By the time you look up the bartender has moved on to the next customer.

•**HOT/COLD-SPOTS** Related to the above is the phenomenon of hot-spots and cold-spots. When a bar is slammed hot-spots will develop. What is happening is the bartender, returning to give the current customer change, will immediately be confronted by the next customer who is standing nearby. When returning with that customer's change there will be another customer standing there waiting for service, etc.

Similarly, there will be cold-spots at the bar that the bartender can't get to because she's caught in a hot-spot. When this happens you can try to move into the hot-spot, but this area is often too crowded to get to. A better bet is to be patient; she's aware that you're there and will get to you as soon as she gets a chance. Hot-spots are broken when a customer pays with an amount that doesn't require change.

•**BARTENDER! BARTENDER!** A contraindicated method of getting the bartender's attention is to yell, "Bartender! Bartender!" while waving your arms frantically. This method will get you noticed, but it won't necessarily get you a drink. It can be very annoying to have someone yelling at you in this manner when you're slammed, plus it's obvious that you're trying to take cuts in the bartender's mental waiting list. No one likes people who cut in line. Also, it's been my experience that customers who act in this manner usually don't have an order ready; when I offer to serve them they turn to their friends to ask what everybody wants... which is precisely the moment I move on to the next customer.

•**THE BARTENDER KEEPS PASSING ME BY** This generally indicates one of two things: 1) You've been stiffing the bartender and he's making you wait. 2) The bartender has determined that you're too drunk to be served and is hoping you leave out of frustration before he has to have *that* conversation with you.

• **BARTENDER TRIAGE** Even if you've been waiting the longest, the bartender may go to someone else before you. Even if you ordered before someone else, the bartender may make their drink first. The reason for this is the bartender is assessing how to serve people the most efficiently and sometimes that means serving a lone guy a pint of beer before she makes several complex drinks for you and your friends.

• **SITTING WITH THE DEAD** Another thing that can slow down your service is to seat yourself at the bar where someone has just vacated and left behind several glasses. Scanning the bar the subliminal image the bartender gets is one of a customer with a drink. This is especially true when the bartender is slammed. The thing to do is to push the glasses into a group and toward the bartender's side of the bar, not so far that they might fall over the edge, but far enough so that the bartender will get the image of dead ones on the bar.

• **CONVERSATION WITH A BARTENDER** People like to talk to bartenders and bartenders like to talk to customers. It's also true that bartenders are there to make a living and other customers want to get a drink. These last two facts take precedence over the first two. If you're in a conversation with a bartender, be ready to hold that thought. Use common sense; if the bar is busy, don't try to involve the bartender in long-winded stories or jokes. If the bartender suddenly begs off in the middle of your story and moves down the bar, don't take it personally.

A bartender's work week is generally much shorter than that of other professions; it is possible to support yourself on a 25-30 hour work week. The other side of the coin is that you can't afford to slack off, even for a minute, at peak business hours. During a typical shift a bartender may make most of his money during two or three peak hours. During that period you've got to be moving at top efficiency or it will cost you money.

It's not just the money it costs you personally, because you're often working with another bartender and pooling tips. One way to get on the bad side of your fellow bartenders is to stand chatting while they do all the work. Then there are your customers. They are impatient when you're slammed, but if you're standing there chatting or are otherwise distracted, they will take it personally.

•**FRIENDS AND LOVERS** This is another sticky subject for bartenders while on duty. If a good friend and/or love interest is sitting at your bar, you want to talk to her but sometimes you can't, for the reasons stated above. Friends and lovers of those in the bar trade have to understand this. Those who need constant attention would do best not to visit their bartender pals during peak hours.

•**NEVER TELL A MEMBER OF THE BAR STAFF TO SMILE.**

•**DON'T BLOCK THE SERVICE STATION** At a busy bar the service station is often also a hot-spot. It's okay to order here so long as you stay alert to the location of the server. When the server approaches you should make way immediately. Servers are often carrying trays heavy with bussed glassware as they approach the service station and they want to put it down as quickly as possible. They also are trying to make a living and the quicker they can give their order to the bartender, the quicker they can deliver their order and come back for another.

If you do order from the service station, get away from it as soon as you receive your drinks. People like to hover around this area, because it's an open area at the bar. But doing so blocks the path of the server and other customers.

•**DON'T CROWD THE FLAP** This is the part of the bar that lifts up.

It can be lowered to extend the bar, but usually it's left up because it's the only way out from behind the bar. There are many reasons bartenders need to come out from behind the bar: Restocking, getting ice, using the restroom, dealing with problems of various sorts. If you're standing there, you're in the way.

•**DON'T TREAT THE GARNISH TRAY AS A SALAD BAR** Some people like to pluck olives or cherries from the garnish tray. If they ask first I always say yes. However, if someone begins grazing on my olives, I'm forced to intervene. I have to spear those olives in advance to save time. If I run low, I have to stop and spear more. This costs me time that could be used to make drinks.

There's also the factor of cleanliness. My hands are quite clean while I'm bartending because I'm washing glasses when I'm not making drinks. The same can't be said for customer's hands, and other customers don't necessarily like to see a lot of different hands on the garnish that may eventually end up in their drinks. For these reasons it's best to keep this behavior to a minimum.

•**BAR KIBBLE** If you need a snack, rather than going for the garnish tray, a better move would be to ask the bartender if she has any bar snacks; peanuts, pretzels, etc. **NOTE:** Whether you buy it from the bar or the bar provides it for free, bar kibble is always salty because salt makes you thirsty and that makes you drink faster.

•**LEAVING DRINKS UNATTENDED** If you must get up and leave your drink unattended, the accepted signal to other customers and the bartender that you plan to return, is to put a serviette (napkin) or some personal item on top of it.

Part of a bartender's work includes busing drinks and making space for the next customer. If the bartender comes to an unattended drink, especially one that is more than half empty, the normal response is to remove it from the bar, wipe the area with a bar rag and ready the space for the next customer. Customers who don't mark their drinks often lose them and/or their seat at the bar and sometimes become annoyed with the bartender, who has simply been doing his job. It's the customer's responsibility to signal the bartender, either verbally or with a serviette, that the drink is still in play. This is especially important in bars where no smoking laws are being enforced as there are many people compelled to leave their drinks at the bar while they go outside for a smoke.

While this method will save your drink and your spot at the bar, it won't do so indefinitely. Depending on how busy the bar is it will generally hold your place and drink from thirty to forty minutes in a slow bar, down to about five or ten minutes in a busy one; a reasonable amount of time to smoke a cigarette or take a squirt. **NOTE:** I don't recommend using a coaster to save your drink. Coasters are used and then reused. Sometimes they fall on the floor. When they do, I pick them up and put them back in the stack of coasters on the bar. Also, they are given to the bar by beer companies and are always imprinted with the company's logo. The ink used in printing tends to impart the smell of ink to your glass. **NOTE:** Some people put a serviette on their drinks when they're finished. Why? I don't know, but I wish they wouldn't because it's confusing.

• **THE BUSSING STATION** Another mistake customers make that causes them to lose their drinks is to set them down on the service station, which is also the bussing station. Any drink showing up here is considered dead and is quickly bussed.

• **THE THOUSAND YARD STARE** The bar is empty, yet the bartender still hasn't come over to ask what you'd like. Instead he stares intently at the wall across from him. You look at the wall, but nothing stands out. What gives? The bartender isn't looking at the wall, he's looking through the wall to a place far, far away… he's having a personal moment. This sometimes happens when business slows to a crawl. The

# Bar Scores

"I got my customers drunk and they
left me all this cool stuff!"
—Jack Yaghubian

bartender sees a way out and takes it, if for only a moment. He'll come around soon, perhaps when you scoot your barstool over and it makes that high-pitched scraping sound.

•**NO LUNCH BREAK FOR THE WICKED** Bartenders can often be found eating behind the bar. This is because their working hours conflict with their eating times or because they have neglected to eat before coming to work. Go ahead, disturb him, he's used to eating in fits and starts… it's part of the job. You may however want to wait until he's done chewing his bite of pizza.

•**BARTENDER'S WORK SPACE** When there's a shift change you may have noticed that the bartender coming on duty will rearrange his work space. With some bartenders the change will be slight, with others the whole work space will be completely rearranged. This doesn't mean that the previous bartender had it wrong, just that each bartender likes his work space set up a bit differently.

•**BLIND SPOTS** Most bars have blind spots caused by things on the bar that block lines of sight. The most common examples are beer towers and garnish trays. Tips or puddles of water behind these obstructions cannot be seen by the bartender until she moves and gains a new perspective. In the case of beer towers, they sometimes block customers from the bartenders line of sight. So if you're sitting with a beer tower between you and the bartender and she hasn't noticed you yet, you might want to stand up.

•**SHIFT CHANGE** The workday in most bars is broken up into at least two shifts. At some point, usually early evening, there is a shift change. It takes a different form in each bar, depending on what their system is, but for most bars and their staff it is a stressful transition. The bartender who's about to be relieved has to get the bar ready for the next bartender. This includes closing out his register, getting ice, making a fresh pot of coffee, restocking the bottled beer, etc. All of this takes him away from making drinks. If you are in a bar when this change occurs be patient. Once the staff has completed the switch they will play catch up until things have settled down. **NOTE:** I have noticed over the years that shortly after the shift change the bar will empty out. There could be a number of reasons for this, but I believe the primary reason is that the shift change reminds those present of how long they have been in the bar. They finish the drink in front of them and leave. The new bartender then has to rebuild a crowd.

- **MARKERS** Sometimes a customer will offer to buy a drink for someone at the bar who has a full drink. Rather than serve the drink immediately, which will wilt before the recipient can get to it, the bartender will take payment for the drink, then put an upside-down shot or rocks glass in front of the person for whom the drink was purchased. This is known as a *marker* and is redeemable by the recipient when they are ready for it (at which point the bartender takes the marker off of the bar). **NOTE:** There are rarely more than one or two markers out at any given time and the bartender is aware of them, so don't try redeeming the shot glass you just emptied for another drink or you'll end up on his shit list.

- **VILLAGE OF THE DAMNED** In just about every bar you enter, the bar itself will have a long-side and a short-end. The short-end is *Village of the Damned*: It's where the regulars sit. The regulars can be recognized by the fact that they drop bottles and other garbage over the side of the bar right into the trash can without looking. Rather than take an empty bar stool there, you'd do better to move down to the long-side of the bar, unless you are one of the regulars.

- **SHAKING THE BARTENDER'S HAND** People often want to shake the bartender's hand, usually upon arrival at or departure from the bar. This is fine, but when the bartender is busy it's not a good idea because both of his hands are in use. At this time it's best to use a visual or verbal form of greeting. **NOTE:** A bartender's hand is usually wet.

•**BEING YOUR OWN SERVER** Serving yourself and your friends from the bar is fine, particularly when there are no servers, but you should know something about how to do it. The most glasses you should attempt to carry at one time is three. You should carry them in a triangular configuration with both hands. Never try to carry four or more because you may drop them before you get to your table.

Occasionally, a customer will ask for a tray to carry an order back to his table. I always deny this request. The last thing I want to see is a customer with a tray of drinks negotiating the distance back to his table.

•**BEING YOUR OWN BUSSER** Bussing your glassware is less of a problem and is appreciated by the bartender, particularly if he's slammed and/or working without a busser. Just make sure that when you set them on the bar you don't put them too near the edge or stack them too high. Personally, I don't like them higher than two glasses. The reason for this is that they become unstable over that height. If they get knocked over, the glasses may break. If they break in the ice well the bartender is going to want to strangle you, so keep this in mind when bussing your own table.

•**HOMELESS PEOPLE** The homeless tend to disrupt business. Because of this they are not welcome in most bars. Some people find this insensitive. They feel the homeless should be treated like anyone else and allowed to remain in a bar if they choose. But these people can get up and leave when they want to and have no responsibility for what happens in the bar. The bartender sees things from a different perspective.

Homeless people need help, none of which is available in a bar. In many cases their homelessness is due to their weakness for the product sold in bars. People who feel strongly about the well-being of a homeless person and believe that a drink will help should take him to their home.

•JUST CAME BY TO HANG OUT Some people mistakenly think a bar is a public facility. They will drop by to sit and relax, ask for water or more often, just to use the restroom. These people are mistaken; bars are private property. They are under no obligation to let the public use their restroom or sit at a table or anything else. What these people are looking for is a public park. NOTE: Most bartenders will let you use their restroom if you ask first. But most bartenders will be annoyed if you just walk past them without a word, use the can, then walk back out. If you do, be prepared for a few choice words on your way out.

•CAMPERS These are the people who buy drinks, but nurse them and/or stay for long periods after finishing them. They also like to spread their personal items around on the bar or the table they occupy. Initially they get hints from the bartender or waiter, which become less subtle and more frequent with the passage of time.

•WI-FI Most bars don't have Wi-Fi, or if they do they don't give out the password. Why? Because Wi-Fi encourages campers.

•BARTENDERS PICKING UP TIPS Some bartender's pick up tips as soon as they hit the bar. Others wait until the customer leaves. This will vary from bar to bar, bartender to bartender, and situation to situation. Personally, I leave them for a while if the customer is sitting at the bar. If it's a customer that came up to the bar for a drink and then leaves, I pick it up. Sometimes I leave the tips for awhile just because I'm busy and could better use the time it would take to pick them up. If it's a regular sitting at the bar I often leave them until she leaves or until she pushes them forward to the edge of the bar, making it clear that they are tips. This shows the regular that I know she's a good tipper and I'm not concerned about it. I'm more likely to pick up tips quickly if they're from people I don't know, especially if they are drinking a lot. In these cases, when they run out of money, they will start buying drinks from their tip pile. I pickup tips as soon as I have a chance on Friday, Saturday and holiday nights.

•**Customers picking up tips:** Unless it's money you've put on the bar, don't ever do this.

•**Making change from tips on the bar** Sometimes people need change and to save time they will make change out of the tips lying on the bar. I wouldn't advise doing this unless you first ask the bartender.

•**The knock** Some bartenders will knock their knuckles on the bar when they pick up tips. This signifies a number of things: First, it's a way to signal that the tip was received and to say thank you. Secondly, it announces that the bartender is collecting a tip, so it won't appear that the bartender is picking up money on the sly. Lastly, it calls the attention of a stiff who is waiting for service, so that he or she will take notice and the hint. This practice is probably derived from card dealers in Las Vegas who knock on the table whenever they take the house cut or a tip.

•**Bartender tendering cash payment** Personally, I do this as soon as the customer hands me cash. But recently I have noticed that some bartenders will leave my money laying on the bar until I'm ready to go. Since this only happens in bars that accept credit cards, I think that some bartenders have gotten so used to taking credit cards and running tabs that they are no longer familiar with taking cash.

Of course there is another explination; the bartender has gotten into the habit of mentally giving out free drinks, but not saying so out loud. When the customer is ready to go, they leave the payment and tip on the bar, which the bartender later puts into the tip jar. Some may do this unconsiously, the habit reinforced by a larger income, but some know exactly what they're doing.

•**Bartender/customer confidentiality** There is no such thing;

anything you do or say can become part of the bartender's repertoire or even an entry in a book like this one. However, when it comes to the regulars, bartenders generally keep things to themselves and other staff members. The activities of the regulars is the bar staff's own private soap opera.

• **BREAKING LARGE BILLS** Customers will sometimes apologize for paying with a large denomination bill. Unless it's a small, neighborhood bar, or a bar that is mismanaged or in bad financial shape, this is not a problem. Fifties and C-notes can be a problem if the bar has just opened or if there has been a shift change and the drawer is new. But this ceases to be a problem within about half an hour after the beginning of the shift. After this, breaking a fifty or a C-note is no different than breaking a twenty, because the bulk of the change will be in the form of twenties. Personally, I would rather customers pay with a large bill, rather than waste time searching their wallet for the correct change.

• **CHECKING $50 AND $100 NOTES** You can expect the bartender to check 50 and 100 dollar notes. It doesn't mean the bartender thinks you're a counterfeiter, he just doesn't know where you got the note. Personally, I've checked C-notes given to me by my boss. **NOTE:** The way to check for a counterfeit is to run your fingernail over the black parts of the bill, like the president's coat. U.S. dollars are printed on an intaglio press which imparts a corduroy effect to the surface. Most counterfeits will be smooth. Another way is to rub the bill between your wet fingers. This will have no effect on genuine bills but on fakes the paper is likely to ball-up. You can also rub the bill over a sheet of newsprint. Genuine bills will leave an ink smudge behind, fakes will not. It's also a good idea to check the water mark because more sophisticated counterfeiters will bleach out five dollar bills on which to print larger denominations. Of course most bartenders will just use the counterfeit detecting pen the boss leaves next to the register, but the other ways make you look cooler.

102

•**YOUR MONEY IS CONFUSING; IT'S ALL THE SAME COLOR** Yes, but there's numbers on it... Forget about colors and read the numbers. It's usually a guy from England who points out that all other countries print their money in different colors for each denomination. It's always me who points out that even if we did print our money in different colors, they wouldn't be the same colors as his money, and thus be just as confusing, perhaps more so. Read the numbers... It's easy!

•**CHANGE** Most bartenders will put your change on the bar, not in your hand. There are two reasons for this: First, it's faster. You can toss it on the bar and immediately move on to the next piece of work. When you put it in someone's hand you have to be a little more genteel, which is slower. The other reason is that when it's tossed on the bar it's there for all to see and fewer disagreements over correct change result. If there is a disagreement, customers sitting nearby may have seen the change as well and can assist in settling the dispute.

•**SHORT CHANGE** Sometimes there is a disagreement as to the denomination of the bill tendered in a bar transaction. This can be problematic. The bartender is usually right; he's probably sober and the customer probably isn't. People can go through money quickly while out drinking and may think they gave the bartender a twenty, when in fact they broke that twenty on their last transaction at another bar.

One method I use to cut down on disagreements is to call out the denomination of the bill as I take it. I always watch as the customer hands the bill over so I know what it is before I take it. As I'm about to put it in the till I look at it again.

I do occasionally make a mistake. When a customer insists he gave me a twenty and I believe he gave me a ten, the first thing I do is to look in the till. If he's right I will find a twenty in the ten slot. If I don't, I tell him he's wrong. Some people will want to argue the point. I'm usually able to convince them otherwise, but on very rare occasions, when I wasn't one-hundred percent certain, I have given the customer the extra ten they feel they deserve. I don't like doing this but sometimes it's the most economical solution for both the bar owner and myself, as a disruption of business during a slammed shift is expensive.

•**ASPIRIN** Most bars will not dispense aspirins to customers, even though they have them on hand for hungover bartenders. The reason for this is that if a person has a bad reaction to the aspirin-alcohol mixture the bar could be sued for illegally dispensing a medicine. However, they aren't responsible if the customer buys their own aspirin, which is why you sometimes see little aspirin packets for sale in bars.

•**SMOKING** It is illegal to smoke in bars in California (and an increasing number of other states and countries). Even though smoking in bars has been outlawed in California since 1998 you can still find the occasional bar where you can smoke. Some use the loophole presented by the law itself, which was speciously written to protect the health of employees, not customers. This being the case, bars with no employees (exclusively owner operated) can legally allow smoking.

Others are just so low profile that they can get away with it for awhile. A bar I like in a seedy part of town used to do this. Then a customer came in slumming one night and was appalled to find, among other things, customers were smoking in the bar! He dutifully reported this on the primary on-line snitch-site. Since then the old ladies who run the bar have been enforcing the smoking ban.

•**E-CIGARETTES** The jury is still out on this one. I don't mind it, but at least one of my co-workers does. In some cities or states it's as illegal as real cigarettes, so it's best to ask before vaping in a bar.

•**POT** Now that marijuana is all but legal, you may feel like asserting your new rights in a bar. But smoking anything in a bar is illegal, so I wouldn't advise lighting up, unless you want to get thrown out.

•**DRUGS** Bartenders generally frown on drug use in their bars because it leads to problems. A person under the influence of a variety of illegal drugs mixed with alcohol makes for customers whose behavior is unpredictable.

•**DRUG DEALERS** If someone is dealing drugs in the bar they are competing with the bartender; every dollar spent on an illegal drug is one less dollar they have to spend on alcohol (It's not much different than a guy bringing a bottle of booze into the bar and selling shots). And while the drug dealer may make money off the bartender's customers, when those same customers have a bad reaction to the drug-alcohol mixture the responsibility falls to the bartender.

•**YOU WANT TO CARD ME?** Invariably the person who complains about being carded (generally in the form of rolled eyes) is a 22 year old woman. The guys don't seem to care and women in their late twenties or older either don't care or are flattered by being carded. The other type of person who takes exception to being carded is a young European of either sex, who always wants to tell you that this is not the case in their home country—as if I didn't know this after hearing about it for over a quarter century. **NOTE:** If you're not prepared to encounter strange laws and customs, don't travel. Stay home.

•**UNDERAGE DRINKERS** Some people who are less than legal drinking age are better behaved drinkers than some people my age (me for instance). However, the law doesn't allow for a case by case basis in terms of who a bartender can legally sell an alcoholic drink. The fines are steep and can affect the entire staff, including the owner. This being the case you can expect the bartender to card you if you have a youthful appearance. **NOTE:** In California there are two primary types of liquor licenses; those where food is a major part of sales (restaurants) and those that sell little or no food (bars). In the latter type a person must be at least 21 years of age just to be in the barroom. In the former type a person of any age can be present, but they still must be at least 21 years old to consume alcohol.

•**ANIMALS IN A BAR** While the law is clear on the matter of under age humans, it's a gray area in the case of animals. I don't believe either has a place in the barroom, but in both cases it's the parent/owner that's the real problem. It never occurs to them that everyone isn't as enthralled by their chattel as they are (see **DANGEROUS BEHAVIOR**).

•**FREE DRINKS** Most bars serve a certain amount of free drinks. The people who get them generally fall into one or more of the following five categories:

**#1** People who work in the bar and restaurant industry (i.e., off-duty bartenders and servers). These people will give you a free drink or even free food when you visit their place of business. They will also recommend your bar to other people if they are well disposed toward it and you, so it behooves both you and the bar owner to take care of them. Hence, a free drink for the bar and restaurant personnel.

**#2** Regulars who spend a lot of money in your bar and help to create its personality. These people add to your cash drawer directly by the money they spend and indirectly by the money they attract in the form of new customers. Hence, a free drink for the regulars.

**#3** High-rollers who come in and spend a lot of money and tip big without being obnoxious about it. You'd like to see more of them and to encourage their return. Hence, a free drink for the high-rollers.

**#4** Sexy people you'd like to sleep with. You'd like to sleep with them, hence, a free drink for the sexy.

**#5** Friends. Hey, they're your friends.

Bartenders have to be careful about free drinks because they can easily get out of hand. It doesn't take long to realize that a free drink usually results in a larger tip and adds greatly to your popularity among the customers. A bartender who takes this route can soon be giving the house away, which results in a larger bottom line for himself at the expense of the bar. For this reason, most bars have a policy regarding free drinks, which can range from quite lenient to absolutely no free drinks at all. In establishments with a rule prohibiting free drinks, the bartenders and servers are required to pay for any drinks they give away.

•**PEOPLE WHO DON'T GET FREE DRINKS** My rule of thumb is that people who expect a free drink don't get one; that goes double for those who ask for a free drink. Stiffs, cheapskates and troublemakers don't get free drinks and neither do the jokers who say that they used to be a bartender. Yeah right, one summer in college for two minutes.

•**BIRTHDAY DRINKS** Free drinks for people on their birthdays isn't a hard-and-fast-rule. If someone is obviously wandering from bar to bar for free birthday drinks and will leave as soon as they've finished their free one and aren't someone you'd want in your bar anyway, they don't get a free drink.

The way to get a free birthday drink is to first order a drink and leave a tip. Then, on your second round, mention that it's your birthday. Most bartenders will give you a free drink at this point, but be prepared to show your I.D.

•**WHERE'S BILL?** If Bill's a friend and you're looking for him this is okay. But if Bill's a staff member, it gives the bartender on duty one of two impressions: **1)** You're disappointed Bill's not behind the bar, perhaps because Bill doesn't charge you for your drinks. **2)** You're fishing for a free drink by giving the impression you're a friend of Bill's. **NOTE:** Most bartenders assume one or both of the above and won't give a free drink to name droppers.

•**Hey, bill only charges me three dollars** Some fools will actually blow their benefactor's cover. This is the way bartenders who are giving the house away get caught.

**Everybody's favorite bartender** How to achieve this distinction is no secret: Bartend drunk and give the house away.

•**Pricing of drinks** The pricing of drinks in a bar is done by management. Good managers try to keep variations to a minimum and use standard up charges. Two examples are; pricing all call liquors the same, even though there is variation in cost per bottle, and a one dollar up-charge for martinis and built drinks. Another convention in pricing is if a drink calls for two or more different alcohols, the drink's price is based on the price of the more expensive alcohol. For instance, when you order a Black Russian you're charged the cost of Kahlúa, unless you order it with Grey Goose vodka, in which case you're charged the cost of Grey Goose.

•**Bartenders in the same bar charge different prices** This is due to confusion or unfamiliarity with the price list, most common during the first week after a price increase, when the bartenders aren't used to the new prices. It's more likely to happen in bars where management has priced drinks with a rigid adherence to cost/profit margin. The result is a myriad of prices, which can be difficult to remember. However, corporate bars, where this pricing scheme is most frequently employed, generally use touch screen registers which cuts down on confusion, since bartenders have to wade through various levels of menus until they find the exact drink with its exact price. In this case management gets its best calculated price per drink... it just sells less of them because bartenders are required to spend so much time wading through menus.

•**Rearranging the bar furniture** It's best to keep this to a minimum. The stools and chairs are where they are for a reason. Moving them can block foot traffic and will get in the way of customers and wait staff. If you do move a chair, don't lift it over your head unless you check first, because there are often things (neon signs, lamps, framed pictures, etc.) above you. A waiter I know, Kate Mata, calls these people, "Road Blockers."

•**SERVIETTES** A.K.A. *Bev-naps* or *cocktail napkins* are used in most bars, primarily because they look more formal than simply setting the drink on the bare bar. But they also serve several other purposes: They dampen the sound of glasses hitting the bar top. They soak up the bar-sweat that forms on the sides of cold glasses and runs down them to form puddles on the bar. They cut down on spilled drinks because the square of paper makes the drink more easily seen, even in peripheral vision.

•**ICE** American bars use a lot of ice. In the U.S. highballs are filled with ice. If you don't like ice in your drink, you must say so before the bartender starts to fill your order. Keep in mind that because highballs are based on the glass being filled with ice first, if you get yours without ice, the glass won't be filled to the usual level. If it were the drink would be weak due a higher proportion of mixer.

•**LIVING ABOVE BARS** People who live above bars have to put up with noise. The reason that the apartment above a bar is for rent is probably because the previous tenants couldn't stand the noise. If you're thinking of moving in above a bar, you should consider this. If you look at the place during the day, it would be wise to come back at night to check the noise level. I have no sympathy for people who move in above a bar and then complain that it's too noisy. The bar was there before you were, and the world doesn't have to conform to your standards. Maybe you should consider moving to the suburbs. Cities tend to be noisy. If every neighborhood in the city were as quiet as a suburb it would be a boring city. And, yes, I live above a bar.

•**HATS IN A BAR (MEN)** I believe you're still required to remove your hat upon entering a church. If you pass through the Hong Kong airport to catch a connecting flight you will come to a large open space where an official looking man in uniform will ask you to remove your hat. I know that in court the bailiff will ask you to remove your hat before the judge enters. In restaurants, if eating at a table, I take my hat off. If I'm eating at the counter, I leave my hat on. But in bars I always leave my hat on

The requirement for men to remove their hats indoors faded away sometime in the 60s. However, you will occasionally encounter a doorman at a club that will inform you that hats are not allowed to be worn inside. This isn't because they are sticklers for outdated manners, but because hats can cause fights in certain crowds. What usually happens is some half-crocked douche/douchette plucks the hat off of a stranger's head to try it on for size. This may amuse the douche/douchette's buddies, but the guy who finds himself hatless takes exception to being the source of their amusement and belts the douche or the douchette's friend. A fight ensues. This no hats rule is rare and the clubs that have it generally aren't worth going into anyway. But for bars, men are not required to remove their hats upon entry and unless you belong to the Art Deco Society or some such thing, it's not considered a breach of etiquette.

•**SHADES IN A BAR** Anyone who wears shades in a bar, except a blind person, is an asshole.

•**TELEVISIONS IN BARS** In sports bars they're fine, since drinking and watching a game is the reason these places exist. But for all other bars they are just blight flickering lights; a needless distraction that stifles conversation.

•**DICE CUPS** Some bars have them, some don't. Some bars may have them when one bartender is working, but not when another is working. The reason for this is that some bartenders don't like the racket dice cups make, so even though there are dice cups in the bar, the bartender will tell you there aren't.

•**LOST AND FOUND** Most bars have lost-and-founds, usually a cubby-hole or drawer. If you lose something in a bar, you will have the best chance of retrieving it if you act as soon as possible after it's lost. The more time that passes, the less likely you are to get it back. The interpretation will be that the owner is either not interested in it or has forgotten where it was lost. Nine times out of ten, people who don't return for a lost item within twenty-four hours won't return at all. Nine times out of ten, valuable items not claimed within forty-eight hours are no longer there to be claimed. However, items with little or no value may lay around for months before they're thrown out.

•**HOW TO AVOID LOSING VALUABLES IN A BAR** If you bring anything of value into a bar, keep it on your person at all times or you risk it being lost or stolen. Don't hang your purse over the back of your chair or barstool and don't leave your phone or wallet on the bar. If it's a large item, keep it in contact with your body so that if someone tries to steal it you will sense movement. Don't leave any garment on a coat rack or otherwise unattended. If you enter a bar during daylight hours wearing shades, take them off and put them in your pocket or purse immediately. People often remove their shades upon entering a bar and, if they leave after it's dark, will forget that they had them until it's too late. It's a similar story for umbrellas during periods of intermittent showers. Book bags and small backpacks are other items that people will put on the floor by their feet and leave behind when they go. **NOTE:** The last time I bought a new pair of shades was over twenty years ago.

•**FINDING MONEY IN A BAR** Generally I would advise a reasonable amount of honesty when it comes to finding valuables in a bar, but money on the floor comes under the old rule: No name, no claim... It's fair game. If you find a twenty on the floor and wave it around asking for the owner, then several are sure to show up. This isn't necessarily dishonesty on the part of your fellow patrons. People in bars spend money more quickly than they realize and may think that dropping a twenty is how they depleted their wad so quickly.

My advice, if you see a bill on the ground, is to pick it up quickly and put it in your pocket. Don't stop to see what denomination it is, don't look around to see if anyone noticed. If people are milling around it and you don't want to attract attention and end up in an argument, you should remove your wallet from your pocket or purse and toss it next to or on top of the bill, then scoop them both up in one motion. Anyone who sees you will assume that you dropped the bill when you dropped your wallet. You may also choose to turn the bill into the bartender on duty, but if you do, be advised that it's going directly into his tip jar.

•**HOW TO AVOID LOSING MONEY IN A BAR** Keep your money in a wallet and file the bills in order of denomination so you will have some idea of what you're pulling out, even after you've had a few drinks. Don't keep your money wadded up in your pocket, as pulling it out will often allow one or more bills to fall to the ground. In fact, if you're tapped-out, the best places to look for that twenty you need to extend your night are along the brass rail at the foot of the bar or in front of the service station where a guy who keeps his money wadded up in his pocket has dropped it.

If you lose your wallet you must act quickly. Notify the bartender and retrace your steps. Try to imagine where the wallet could have been kicked by a passerby. People aren't all that observant so your wallet may lie unnoticed for some time. Check the trash cans in the restrooms. People who find or steal a wallet will want to strip it of its cash and credit cards as soon as possible and they will want to do so unobserved. Once they have the money they will dispose of the evidence. Because this person could be of either gender, both restrooms should be checked. Of course, your cash and credit card will be gone by the time you find your wallet in a trash can in the restroom, but at least you will have your wallet and I.D.

•**How to avoid losing a credit card in a bar** Don't use it, pay with cash. Every bar I have worked in that accepts plastic has always had a glass, a box or a drawer containing wads of forgotten credit/debit cards. What these people do for money the rest of the night or the next day, I don't know. I guess they have several cards. Sometimes these people call to see if they left their card at my bar. I never look through the stack of forgotten credit cards; I have better things to do. I simply tell them they have to come by the bar and look through the stack for themselves.

•**Telephone** While requests to use the bar phone have become all but non-existent, it does occasionally happen that someone has lost their phone, it's been stolen or it has died and no charger is available. In this situation the old rule still applies: Never use the bar phone without first asking the bartender if it's okay. The bar phone is meant for bar business, but sometimes the bartender will let a customer use the bar phone for a quick, local call. However, don't presume this to be the case.

•**Paging Customers** This stopped about the time cell phones came into common use. If you call a bar expecting to page a friend you suspect is there, you'll probably be disappointed by the bartender's response.

•**Smart phones** These are a fact of modern life, but they can be a nuisance. The man or woman sitting next to you may not want to hear one-half of the details of your life. Luckily texting has largely replaced talking on these devices. However, if/when voice recognition becomes the norm, the drone of one sided conversations that were a hallmark of the late 20th and early 21st centuries, will resume, except this time around the conversation will be in the form of voice commands/dictations shouted into a phone.

•**CHARGING SMART PHONES/CELL PHONES** Most bar workers don't mind doing this if they aren't busy and if they have an available outlet. Some bar workers may not provide this service because they don't want to take responsibility for your expensive electronic device while it's charging behind the bar (if that's where the outlet is). Keep in mind, whatever type of phone you have, you'll probably have to provide your own charging cable.

•**SOCIAL MEDIA** It's not uncommon for a couple to enter the barroom and come up to the bar to order their drinks, never stopping their incessant key strokes. After receiving their drinks they move to a table where both settle down to become blue faced zombies. Often they finish their drinks and leave with few if any words exchanged between themselves or others in the bar. It makes me wonder why they bothered to come into the bar at all or why they're together.

•**LOOK HOW CUTE (OR UGLY, DISGUSTING, OR COOL, ETC.)** Yet another example of annoying behavior involving smart phones is that people now regularly want to shove their phone in your face and have you consider mundane images of their puppy, their kitten, their baby, their previous night's dinner, some naked chick... Just about anything. Yawn.

•**BAR APPS** Perhaps the most frightening prospect is the expected arrival of apps that allow customers to order drinks and pay for them with their smart phones and other devices. Nothing spells doom for the bar industry more than what some software engineer and a banker think the bar industry needs.

•**FRIDAY AND SATURDAY NIGHTS** The worst time to go drinking in a bar is on Friday and Saturday nights and several of the holidays, like Saint Patrick's Day and New Year's Eve.

•**HOVERING** On busy nights people will use a technique called *hovering* to get a seat at the bar or at a table. While it is permissible to do so, try not to be too obvious or to act impatient as you will annoy what are, after all, your benefactors.

•**DIFFERENT BARS HAVE DIFFERENT EXPECTATIONS** Just as you're expected to act differently at your mother's house than at your best friend's house, different bars have different expectations of behavior from their customers. In some you can yell, spill beer on the floor, lead your posse in a group sing-a-long of sea chanties at the top of your lungs and otherwise act up. But in some bars you are expected to rein in your more expansive tendencies and you can generally sense this upon entry. Ignore what good sense tells you at your own risk.

•**BAR ECOLOGY** Cutting down on waste is a concern in all sectors of modern life and bars are no exception. For example, most bars these days separate their trash into bottles and other sorts of garbage. In San Francisco this has become the law, in other places it's economics. It costs money to have trash collected and the charge is based on the volume that must be collected each week. Since well over half of all garbage generated by a bar consists of bottles, cans and cardboard, bars can cut down on their trash collection bill if they isolate this waste. It is then collected by recyclers, who charge nothing for their service because they plan to sell what they collect.

Customers can also help to cut down on waste. One way customers contribute to needless waste in a bar comes in the way that they deal with spills. When a customer spills a drink he will grab the nearest thing handy to wipe it up, which tends to be a large wad of serviettes. The best way to deal with spills is to use a bar rag, but I would advise that you ask a member of the staff first before grabbing a rag off the bar. Some bars have a low supply of clean bar rags and bartenders covet the clean, dry ones which they hang on their apron string or from a belt loop and use it to dry their hands. A bartender who is used to having a relatively clean bar rag in a bar where clean rags are at a premium, will not like to see one of the clean ones used to wipe up a spill on the floor. If asked for a rag the bartender will, most likely, produce a really grungy one from behind the bar. This is a rag that has already been cycled through its usage from the clean, dry one on his waist to the rolled or folded damp one on the bar, to its current position of filthy mess for wiping up spills on the floor. **NOTE:** Actually the very best thing to use for wiping up spills on the floor is old newspapers, but few are found in bars anymore.

•**CODE OF THE BAR RAG** You may have noticed that while some bartenders wear their bar rag hanging off the back of their waist band or apron string, others wear it on the side or in the front. You may also have concluded that this is arbitrary or simply personal taste. You're wrong. Actually there is a defined code concerning where the bartender wears his/her bar rag: If it's in the back, that indicates this bartender is in a committed relationship (off-limits). If it's worn on the side this indicates the bartender is in a relationship, but likes *strange stuff* on occasion or is in a quarrel with his/her partner (caution). But when it's worn in the front this indicates that the wearer is a full-service bartender (full speed ahead!).

# Ribbed, for her pleasure.

*What a Gentelman used to be expected to do for a Lady*

# What a Man is compelled to do for a Woman

*Then*

# Now

# Nature's Call

**IN EVERY BAR THERE ARE USUALLY** two restrooms and what goes on in them often exceeds their intended uses. These excesses may include smoking, snorting and injecting drugs, taking baths in the sink, lover's quarrels, sexual encounters of various descriptions, changing clothes, etc. Bartenders prefer the use of these rooms to be confined to their intended use, but it's difficult to keep an eye on what goes on because they are hidden away and often have locks on them, which is the reason they are chosen for said activities in the first place. One way to keep these sorts of activities to a minimum is not to put a lock on the door, but then other problems arise: Complaints from customers, primarily female, about the lack of privacy.

This concern over the customer's use of the restrooms has nothing to do with prudishness and everything to do with the smooth operation of a bar. *You don't buy beer, you rent it*, and people won't keep renting their beverage of choice if they can't make room for more.

•**MEN VS. WOMEN** There are differences between the way men and women make use of the rooms set aside for them. Men's rooms smell worse. Maybe that's just my opinion because I'm a man and prefer the smell of women, but I think it has to do with the fact that men tend to miss the target, especially when they're drunk. To be fair, I must point out that it isn't easy to hit such a small target as a toilet bowl with a high pressure hose; which is why urinals were invented—they make aiming unnecessary. Men also tend to spend a lot less time in this room. Washing hands and primping in the mirror is just a waste of time when there's all that beer to drink. **NOTE:** You will rarely find a mirror in the men's room. Why? Because when men get drunk and strikeout with the ladies they tend to punch mirrors, which breaks them.

Women, on the other hand, seem to camp out in the women's room. They like to draw or write with lipstick on the mirror, and they seem to enjoy blotting their lipstick on the walls. They also tend to use an enormous amount of toilet paper and hand towels. Women will come up to the bar and complain when the women's room runs out of toilet paper or hand towels; men rarely do. At the end of the night when I'm cleaning up, the wastebasket in the men's room is rarely full, while the wastebasket in the women's room is always overflowing onto the floor. This may indicate a greater ecological awareness on the part of men, but somehow I feel that's a misreading of the evidence.

Finally, there's the matter of the toilet seat. In the women's room it's always down while in the men's room it's always up. In bars that have mixed-use restrooms, this can be a source of annoyance for the female customers.

To the males I would say, if there's a female next in line behind you, you may want to put the seat down when you're finished. To the females, I would like to point out that if the seat is up when you enter, think of this as an assurance that the male before you didn't piss on it. Often, rather than wasting time lifting the seat in a public restroom, men will simply piss over it and let the last few drops fall where they may. That's the reason toilet seats in many public restrooms have a gap in the front.

But as female co-workers of mine have pointed out over the years, men aren't the only ones who piss on the toilet seat. Due to the growing germaphobic tendencies in our culture, women tend to hover when using the toilet in a public restroom. This practice results in urine all over the seat which is left for the next woman in line. As one of my female co-workers says: *If you piss like a man, raise the seat like a man.*

•**VOMITING** This is another valid use of the restrooms and as messy as it can be, due to the fact that people tend to be bad shots when they're yaking, it is still preferable to other locations for this activity.

If you have to throw up, please use the toilet or the waste basket, <u>not the sink</u>. If you throw up in the sink it will clog and the bartender will be forced to scoop your vomit out with his hands.

Unfortunately, people don't always make it to the restroom. Perhaps it's due to long lines which preclude a timely entrance, or simply waiting until it's too late. Whatever the reason, people will throw up just about anywhere in a bar: In a corner, in front of the restroom door, on the restroom door, on a wall, on the bar, on another customer, or on a member of the bar staff. I've never seen anyone throw up on the ceiling, but I've only been bartending since 1986. Ah, the glamorous life of a bartender.

# The Mating Game

**B**ARS ARE PLACES WHERE people meet other people with whom they form relationships, most of which are strictly friendships, but others are of a romantic nature. These can be of the opposite or same sex variety, but as I am writing this from the perspective of a straight bartender in a primarily straight bar, it is the relationships of the male/female sort on which I will now comment.

•ACCEPTING DRINKS FROM STRANGERS When someone you don't know sends you a drink in a bar, it's rarely just a drink they're sending, it's also a message: *I want to meet you,* or *I'm sitting here admiring you,* or *I have money to spend, are you impressed?,* or *I'm lonely, come talk to me.* Essentially, *I want something from you.*

•MEN BUYING WOMEN DRINKS From what I've seen I would advise that unless you know the woman in question, save your money. Men who send drinks to women sitting at the other end of the bar with whom they have had no previous contact, are fools. Even fools get lucky, but generally you're just throwing your money away and making yourself the object of ridicule by the very woman you're trying to impress.

This practice can also cause problems for the bartender, as some women will be offended by an unordered drink set before them, suspecting that the sender will feel he's earned her attention and will soon be moving over to talk with her.

The way I deal with this is to ask the woman first if she wants the drink and indicate the fellow who is offering to buy it. If she says, "Yes," I serve it. If her response is, "No," I tell him that his offer was declined. This saves me the trouble of breaking up an uncomfortable situation later.

Of course, there's always the joker who insists that I serve her anyway. This is a guy who has more money than sense. My response to his insistence can be inferred from the section entitled: *Who's in charge here?*

•**WOMEN BUYING MEN DRINKS** This is rare. Women do, of course, buy male friends drinks, but here we're talking about a case where the two people concerned have little or no previous contact. This situation doesn't present much possible trouble for the bartender and when I receive such a request I generally comply. Men usually find this flattering, because it's something that doesn't happen often. However, keep in mind that some men will interpret this sort of overture in the same way they would if they were the ones sending the drink: An invitation for sex. Not all men will read the situation this way, but the ones that do are the ones most likely to come scampering over to your side in an amorous mood.

•**MEN ACCEPTING DRINKS FROM WOMEN** When a woman sends you a drink, you must remember that women are often more subtle in their approach to the mating game than men and will interpret signals differently. While this move is almost certainly an invitation to come over and talk with her, you would be well advised to approach her gingerly. If you swagger up acting as if sex is a foregone conclusion, you're likely to lose out. If you really botch it you could end up with a second free drink, the one you'll be wearing as you slouch back to your bar stool. The best approach is to walk over, thank her for the drink and see where the ensuing conversation leads. Remember, she's the one who stuck her neck out and sent the message that she wanted to talk, now she wants to interview you. If you pass the test and sex is on her mind, she'll eventually make that clear.

•**WOMEN ACCEPTING DRINKS FROM MEN** If you have no interest in speaking with the man offering to buy you a drink, your best and most honest course of action is to decline it, because it's likely that soon after you've taken the first sip of that drink he'll be standing at your side, chatting you up. Of course, you can take the position that if someone wants to buy you a drink that's his problem, and that you can accept it and not owe him a thing. In other words, you can play dumb and act as if you believe that a stranger would give you something for nothing. This is a game I wouldn't advise playing because it can often lead to more trouble than the drink is worth. I should add here that in such cases I am less likely to intervene on behalf of the woman if she seems annoyed by the new attention she's receiving. My feeling is that she was complicit in causing the problem and she can get herself out of it—that's the price of a free drink.

•**MEN ACCEPTING DRINKS FROM MEN** This is primarily the case where the two men know one another, but I usually ask before serving the drink. Sometimes the man being offered the drink will refuse because he has other commitments, perhaps he wants something different for his next drink, or maybe he feels he's had enough for the night. The same goes for women accepting drinks from women.

•**BARTENDERS AS SEX OBJECTS** It's no secret that bartenders meet a lot of people or that they tend to be promiscuous. This is simply due to the nature of the job; bartenders are the focal point of the bar because they're the ones you must go to for a drink, thus they are accessible. Being the focus of what is essentially a party, it's as if the bartender's on stage, which lends excitement to his persona. Working in such a public setting also gives the person who is entertaining an interest in the bartender certain important bits of information; he's employed and he's connected to a community in which he is an important and visible member, so he is not likely to be an ax-murderer. Plus, with a little bit of homework his schedule can be ascertained, so he's easy to find.

On top of this, because a bar is a place where singles tend to congregate in the hopes of meeting other like-minded individuals, there is a high percentage of available singles in the bar at any given time, particularly in the evening. The fact that everyone in a bar is probably drinking alcohol, which lowers inhibitions as it heightens amorous ambitions, rounds out the picture. Given all this, it's easy to see why bartenders, on average, aren't good choices for those seeking long-term relationships. The temptations are great, and while opportunity may knock but once, temptation will bang on the door for years.

•**FULL-SERVICE BARTENDERS** On the other hand, if you're just looking for a one or two night hook-up with no strings attached, a bartender can be an excellent choice.

•**AMOROUS MOODS** Occasionally two customers will decide that kissing one another would be a good idea. There's nothing wrong with this, up to a point. But when it goes on for longer than five or ten minutes and reaches the level of serious face sucking and body groping, it will begin to annoy those nearby.

•**NUDITY** This is generally the domain of inebriated women who want to get attention by exposing prized body parts, usually breasts. Some will pretend they're doing a bar trick and affix matches to their nipples, which they then light on fire. Others use the ploy of showing off a tattoo that's in a private place. But most simply pull up their shirt and flash the bar.

This sort of behavior usually annoys the other women at the bar and may earn the exhibitor admiring hoots from the men, so it does work to that degree. But it also makes the woman in question the butt of a few jokes before everyone returns to what they were doing before.

If she persists in this behavior the bartender will generally put a stop to it because it can lead to thinning of the bar population, as the women begin to leave with their men in tow. Or it can lead to trouble if one or more of the simpler fellows in the bar feel her displays are meant to attract him to her side.

•COITUS ANYONE? On rare nights two customers will decide that sexual intercourse with one another, in a bar, is a good idea. This is never a good idea. I have seen couples pull it off with some amount of discretion, but for the most part it's two people who are way too drunk to be out in public. It's time to go home, or at least to a motel.

•MATING SEASON The mating season for humans begins on the 31st of October, Halloween, and runs until the 21st of December, the Winter Solstice. This is the period of the year in which couples are most likely to form.

# Harassment

**B**ARS ARE SOCIAL PLACES The social interaction that takes place therein, fueled by and sometimes encumbered by alcohol, generates arguments, disagreements and transgressions of various sorts. Occasionally these situations cross the line of acceptable behavior into the realm of harassment.

•MEN HARASSING WOMEN Overzealous men, often drunk and either misreading signals, or simply signal-illiterates are the most frequent offenders. If a woman is being harassed by a male customer it's important that she make this clear to the man who's annoying her. Her best course of action is to move to another area of the bar. If that isn't convenient, or if the man follows her, then she should let the offending party know that she would prefer to be left alone. Subtlety rarely works, so be direct. If that doesn't work, it's time to bring the bartender into the picture. Once you've established the fact that this person is bothering you, the bartender is in a much better position to help.

Some women, when confronted with this situation, will continue to engage in polite conversation with the offending male while making pleading glances at the bartender in hopes of an intervention. This puts the bartender in the awkward position of seeming to make a value judgment of the situation; it personalizes his involvement. This is especially true if the bartender is a male, in which case he may be viewed by the offending male customer as a rival, perhaps a *White Knight* who is himself trying to make points with the woman. This is a bad situation as it can lead to a physical confrontation, which is sometimes required in a bartender's line of work, but due to the disruption of business, the possibility of physical injury and/or legal ramifications is always best avoided.

If, on the other hand, the woman has clearly established the fact that she doesn't appreciate the attention of the offending male, the bartender can then intervene as a neutral third party whose job it is to maintain order. The offending male may at this time direct a dirty look or a few choice words at the bartender and/or the woman in an attempt to save face, but that's usually as far as it will go.

•**WOMEN HARASSING MEN** This is less common than the above situation and less problematic, at least in terms of its ability to cause problems and disruptions. But occasionally it does get out of hand and when it does it can present some special problems, particularly if the bartender is male. It doesn't look good for a male bartender to physically eject a female customer. Additionally, he can't use the full range of force that he would against a man. And there generally aren't female customers standing around waiting to get into a barroom brawl (i.e., back-up) the way there often is with male customers. In such a situation, you're pretty much on your own, limited to grabbing her arms and moving her towards the door as best you can, which is fine if you're much bigger and stronger than she is, but if she's near your size and resorts to screaming, biting and kicking, it can get ugly.

There is another form of female-on-male harassment which takes place when a woman feigns sexual interest in a man, either for her own ego gratification, to get a free drink, or for the entertainment of herself and/

or her friends. This is a far more subtle and intractable situation for the bartender. For one thing society allows for a wide range of behavior in this area and the line that separates innocent from dangerous behavior is fuzzy at best. The bartender who suspects trouble may erupt is forced to make a value judgement, knowing that he could be mistaken (perhaps the woman really does have an interest in this fellow), or to simply ignore it and hope he is wrong. This behavior is potentially as dangerous as other forms of harassment. For instance, if she plays this game with more than one male, or if the bartender gets mixed up in it, it may result in a fight.

•MEN HARASSING MEN An argument over a woman, an argument over nothing at all; this situation requires quick attention by the bartender before it escalates to the point where a physical intervention is required. While the same rules apply here as in other cases of harassment, this situation can quickly deteriorate to a point where reason has no effect. This is especially true when the two fellows involved have a strongly developed sense of masculine propriety. If separating the two individuals by way of reason fails and an altercation seems imminent, the bartender will generally take a quick inventory of the available muscle in the room and direct it to the problem in the hopes of averting a fight or, if one is already underway, to break it up. Both persons responsible for the disruption will often be ejected, regardless of *who started it*.

•WOMEN HARASSING WOMEN This usually remains on the verbal level. Cat fights are rare in my experience, at least since I left high school. Some men claim they enjoy a good cat fight. I would guess that the phenomenon of female mud wrestling gets its appeal from this male fascination with women fighting women. I believe this interest stems from the possibility of one or both of the contestants being partially disrobed during the heat of battle. While I'll confess to a healthy interest in partially disrobed females, I prefer to witness them without the benefit of other spectators and under somewhat calmer conditions.

•CUSTOMERS HARASSING THE BARTENDER This ranges from the annoy-

131

ing yackety-yack of drunks, repeating their endless stories, to outright hostility. In the case of drunks, bores and head melters the bartender will escape by finding other work to do, or if it's slow, rely on occasional head nodding and uttering "yeah...yeah" at appropriate intervals. Hostile customers simply get cut off and shown the door.

•**DEATH THREATS** While rare, occasionally a customer who has run afoul of the bartender will threaten to come back and kill him. In more than a quarter century of bartending I personally have had a half dozen such threats. I never take these guys seriously, though I do watch my back and the front door for the rest of the night, just to be on the safe side. The guys that worry me are the ones who say nothing and leave in a silent, smoldering rage.

•**YOU'LL HEAR FROM MY LAWYER** I've never heard from anybody's lawyer.

•**CUSTOMERS HARASSING THE COCKTAIL WAITRESS** Many men are attracted to cocktail waitresses. This is partially due to the fact that cocktail waitresses are women in a bar who appear to be alone. They are also generally attractive women, as bar owners know that an attractive woman will hold the attention of male customers longer than an unattractive one.

On the other hand, these women aren't there to meet men, but to make a living. Some waitresses who aren't interested in advances from male customers will wear a fake wedding ring to advertise themselves as off-limits, but as this is fairly common knowledge, men will often ignore wedding rings on waitresses. What these men fail to grasp is that while these women may not be married, by wearing the ring they are signifying that they aren't interested in advances from male customers. It's worth mentioning here that one of the quickest ways to get yourself ejected from a bar is to insult, touch, pinch or otherwise harass a cocktail waitress.

# *AutoRace to the Rescue*

### By RUBEN DANN

A milestone was passed in New York City this week, just in time for St. Patrick's Day, with the opening of AutoRace; a completely automated Retail Alcohol Consuming Establishment (R.A.C.E.).

The way AutoRace works is simple; a customer goes to AutoRace.com and places an order on his or her telescreen. Payment for the drink is automatically deducted from the customer's PayPal or BitCoin account.

On one wall of AutoRace is a bank of chutes which are covered by protective plastic doors. Behind this wall is a maze of tubes controlled by a computer that directs precise amounts of alcohol and other ingredients into a mixing vessel in which the drink is mixed before being served in the proper glass. All of this is accomplished much faster, with more precision and hygiene than a human being could manage.

A moment after a drink is ordered it appears under a numbered chute, the number corresponding to a number texted to the customer's telescreen. When the customer waves his or her telescreen near the sensor above the chute, the plastic door springs open allowing the drink to be collected.

A decade ago few would have predicted this. Then five years ago all fast food outlets switched to automated delivery systems. Four years ago Starbucks introduced its now famous Automat Cafés. And last year ordering and paying with a telescreen device became the norm in bars; tipping ended overnight and most of the bartenders left town for greener pastures.

Since then bar owners have spent their days headhunting new bartenders. By now everyone in New York is familiar with the listings for, "Bartender wanted, minimal experience required," on Craigs's List and the, "Bartender wanted, inquire within during business hours," signs posted on virtually every bar in The City. All of this is due to the fact that the average turnover rate for bartenders in New York City is now fifty-nine days, according to the New York Bar and Restaurant Association.

Enter AutoRace; no bartenders required. On the night we attended there were only three employees present, the bouncer, a harried busser, and the greeter, an older gentleman who wouldn't discuss his compensation or his job qualifications, though he did tell us that his last employer was Walmart.

The room itself was comfortable; soft muzak floated through the tastefully decorated and dimly illuminated interior. Scattered about were over stuffed chairs and sofas in which the customers sat, their faces bathed in the soft glow of their telescreens. Conversation in the AutoRace was minimal, limited to our interview of the greeter and his constant, "Welcome to AutoRace" or "Good night and thank you for drinking at AutoRace," which were his only duties.

Occasionally a customer would get up and go to the bank of chutes to retrieve a drink. Our attempts to interview customers were met with detached, confused stares and/or dismissive waves of hands as they quickly returned their attention to their telescreens.

FutureRace Inc., the owners of AutoRace, informed us in a texted response to our queries, that ten additional locations are under construction in New York City and environs. In the text they also predicted that AutoRace would quickly become the standard model for bars, or R.A.C.E.s to use their terminology, in The City and beyond.

# Trouble Makers

**B**ARS ARE LIKE GARDENS; if you don't weed them, the weeds take over. This being the case, experienced bartenders check out each new customer as they enter the bar. This isn't always possible, as bartenders are often concerned with various tasks, but other factors permitting, they will check you out. The reason for this is that they want to know who's in his or her bar and to be ready for trouble before trouble is ready for them.

What they're looking for is anyone who stands out from the crowd, anyone who looks angry or otherwise disturbed, and/or anyone who has caused trouble in the past. If they see someone they suspect of being a potential problem they will alert the other members of the staff so they can all check him out until he's deemed no threat.

SOME PROBLEMS ARE APPARENT FROM THE GET-GO:

•A KNOWN PERSON WHO'S BEEN **86'D**, A HOMELESS PERSON, ANY-

ONE OPENLY SOLICITING ANYTHING, AN OBVIOUSLY DERANGED, DRUGGED OR DRUNK PERSON

**OTHERS ARE LESS APPARENT, BUT HERE ARE SOME TIP-OFFS:**

•**PEOPLE WHO WANDER SLOWLY ABOUT THE ROOM BUT MAKE NO ATTEMPT TO BUY A DRINK OR LOCATE FRIENDS,** particularly if they are carrying a newspaper. This is the M.O. of a sneak thief looking for an unattended purse, wallet or cash. The newspaper is used to hide the loot as he takes to the street.

A newer take on this was illustrated to me a few years ago: The thief entered the bar chatting on his cell phone. He continued chatting as he wandered the barroom, which is a great cover because people often look about and wander aimlessly when talking on a cell phone. But this fellow wasn't the least bit aimless: He soon located a wallet, which he grabbed out of an unattended purse, then fled the bar before he could be caught.

•**PEOPLE WHO GO IN AND OUT OF THE BAR REPEATEDLY** This behavior is often associated with drugs; either the sale, purchase or use thereof. Other times it's just a mentally ill or deranged person. In either case they can present a problem for the bartender. In states with a no-smoking law, these people are now often lost in the tide of smokers; leaving the bar to smoke, then coming back in to drink. The difference is that smokers go out, they smoke a cigarette, then return to their drink in the bar.

The potential trouble makers come in, then leave. They come back in and order a drink. They then put the drink down and go out again. They return, take a sip, look about nervously and go back out. This difference quickly becomes obvious to the bartender who, along with the regulars, will watch them until they finally leave for good.

•**A PERSON WHO ANNOUNCES THAT HE HASN'T HAD A DRINK IN A**

**YEAR (OR ANY LONG SPAN OF TIME)** What is implied in this announcement is that this person has a drinking problem and has been forced to quit. However, he has now decided to fall off the wagon and has chosen your bar in which to do it. Lucky you.

•**OLD PEOPLE** Old people have had longer to develop their bad habits, yet their bodies are in a deteriorating state. I'm always nervous when a person my age or older, that I don't know, is drinking in my bar. I've had to call an ambulance for aged customers more than once over the years.

•**PEOPLE WHO HOP FROM TABLE TO TABLE TALKING TO STRANGERS** This could be someone trying to buy or sell drugs or it could just be an annoying person. Either way, he's not good for the bar.

•**PEOPLE WHO RUN IN TO ESCAPE A PURSUER** I understand that they want to be around as many people as possible when someone is chasing them with intent to do them bodily harm, but they aren't someone I'm happy to see.

•**A PERSON WHO COMES IN AND ORDERS,** "The cheapest beer you got," then complains that it's too expensive.

•**ONE FOR THE ROAD** A person who says, "One more, then I'm gone," soon followed by, "One more, then I'm gone," again and again until you finally have to show them the door.

•**A PERSON WHO ORDERS A SIMPLE DRINK,** like a gin and tonic, then after a couple of sips pushes it away, saying with a scowl, "I can't drink this, give me something else." This is a person with a problem in his life, probably at work where his boss has yelled at him or maybe fired him. Now he's on a mission to find someone who's even worse at their job than he is at his. A bartender is an easy target. I always give him something else; a refund and an explanation that I don't feel that I'll be able to please him. Fact is, nobody will be able to please him.

•**PEOPLE WHO MAKE OTHERS NERVOUS OR UNCOMFORTABLE**

137

- PEOPLE WHO ARE ESPECIALLY SULLEN OR WITHDRAWN OR WHO ARE OVERLY ANIMATED OR WHO ARE OVERLY FRIENDLY/ENTHUSIASTIC TO PERFECT STRANGERS

- PEOPLE FAR YOUNGER OR FAR OLDER THAN THE AVERAGE AGE GROUP THAT FREQUENTS THE BAR

- PEOPLE WHO APPEAR TO BE FAR BELOW OR FAR ABOVE THE AVERAGE INCOME LEVEL OF THOSE WHO FREQUENT THE BAR

- PEOPLE WHO ARRIVE IN STRETCH LIMOS OR PARTY BUSES

- PEOPLE IN BIZARRE OR OUTLANDISH COSTUMES

- THE ABOVE TIP-OFFS ARE NOT DEFINITE INDICATORS OF TROUBLEMAKERS, but they are indicators of possible trouble and most bartenders will keep an eye on them until their suspicions are proved wrong.

If I sense trouble is brewing and there's no back-up, such as regulars or a doorman, I search the bar for the biggest guy sitting at the bar and throw him a free drink. This will insure that he's around if/when trouble erupts and that, presumably, he's well disposed toward me and that he has my back.

- EVERYONE SHOULD BE GIVEN BENEFIT OF THE DOUBT It will cause trouble and embarrassment to all involved if a bartender acts prematurely on his assumptions and he's proved wrong. When the line of acceptable behavior is crossed will vary from bar to bar and from bartender to bartender. What doesn't vary is that reading people, assessing situations that arise between people, making a judgment call as to when the line of acceptable behavior has been crossed and by whom, and then dealing effectively and fairly with the situation is the most difficult part of bartending.

# Simple Is The New Smart

# Just Do It!

# Dangerous Behavior

**D**UE TO POOR JUDGMENT, absence of mind or drunkenness, customers, or even bar staff, will occasionally do things which put themselves and/or others in danger. Beyond not wanting to see someone get hurt, there are legal ramifications: Persons hurt on bar premises can and will sue for damages. Courts often take the side of the plaintiff, even if the plaintiff admits to being drunk, because the bar and the bartender are considered responsible for creating his drunken state. This being the case, bartenders will strive to avoid preventable accidents. Below are some of the more common hazards.

•PUTTING EMPTY GLASSWARE WHERE IT SHOULDN'T BE Customers deposit glasses wherever they happen to be standing at the time their glasses become empty. This can be dangerous when the glass is left on the floor of a crowded bar where someone can step on it.

•PUTTING FULL GLASSWARE WHERE IT SHOULDN'T BE Customers aren't as likely to abandon a full glass as an empty one, but it does happen and can be just as dangerous. They will sometimes place a drink near the edge of a table, where it can be knocked off onto the floor. An additional danger created by full glassware is the contents, which when spilled on the floor can create a slipping hazard for other customers.

•**PUTTING CUSTOMERS WHERE THEY DON'T BELONG** Sometimes customers will get up on a barstool, tabletop or even the bar itself. The offenders are usually, but not always, women. Drunk women in high heels. Injury followed by a lawsuit is a distinct possibility here, so most bartenders will put a stop to it quickly.

•**DANCING** It's fine if there's room for it, but in crowded bars dancing can present a hazard because servers and other customers must negotiate the tight spaces between people in the bar. Flying glassware is often the result of dancing in tightly packed barrooms.

There's also the legal issue; an occasional couple dancing to a favorite song isn't a problem, but the whole room gyrating every night will eventually attract the attention of the local authorities. So far as I know, all states in the U.S. require a dance hall permit to promote and allow dancing in their establishments. To qualify for one bar owners must fill out a form describing square feet of their establishment, the number of exits, etc. The law is enforced by the fire marshal whose job it is, among other things, to avoid headlines describing the fiery death and injury of scores of people trapped in a burning building with too few fire exits for the size of the crowd.

•**HORSE PLAY** Wrestling and other feats of strength, throwing things across bar to get someone's attention, spraying or sloshing beer from a bottle onto friends, etc. A little bit of this is okay, but when it gets to the point of two guys rolling around on the barroom floor or glasses knocked off the waitress's tray by a projectile or people slipping in a puddle of beer (preferably before this stage is reached) I put a stop to it.

•**CHILDREN** Occasionally, customers will want to bring a child, usually a very young child, with them into a bar. Their reasoning is that an infant obviously isn't going to be drinking and that no A.B.C. agent or cop would bust a bar for an underage customer in such a case. The problem is that bars can be dangerous places for adults, so they will be even more so for infants. The possible scenarios are numerous and horrifying. The excuse that the parents said they would take all responsibility won't cut it with the judge who presides over the law suit, brought by those same parents, anymore than it will with the insurance company.

Visitors from Europe are confused by this, as the laws are different in their home countries. **AS ELSEWHERE NOTED:** If you're not prepared to encounter strange laws and customs, you shouldn't travel.

•**ANIMALS** It's against the Health Code, but that's the least of the problems associated with animals in a bar. Dogs are the primary offenders, but dog-owners love to bring their pets with them. They will assure you that their dog wouldn't hurt a fly. Then someone inadvertently steps on or kicks the animal and it reflexively bites a customer. Or, the dog finds a comfortable place to lie down, which just happens to be in the path of an inebriated customer who trips over the animal. The owner's assurances of safety leave with them and their chattel and the bar is stuck with a lawsuit.

Unfortunately, some years ago it became law that people can get an *emotional support animal* license for any animal, for any reason, which allows them to bring said animal into a bar or other establishment. Any animal they deem necessary for their own comfort and well being; a Pit Bull or a giraffe, it doesn't matter in the eyes of the law. If confronted about their animal they will tell you it's a service animal.

Of course the law not only allows, but compels bartenders to refuse service to any person they feel is a danger to themselves or others— also for any reason. My way of dealing with these people is to tell them, "Oh a service animal. Okay, that's different. But I refuse service to you." If they ask why I tell them, "I believe you've been over-served." When they protest I tell them, "I do make mistakes, and you're welcome to get a second opinion from a bartender down the street." If they persist I tell them, "Well, now that I've said that I believe you're drunk, I could be in legal trouble if anything happens to you." (I have no idea if that's true, but I figure they don't either).

Another tack I once used was to ask the dog's master for his identification. When he asked me "Why?" I explained to him that we needed know who to sue to cover our losses, in case his dog bites or trips someone.

The animal isn't the problem, it's the owners who are the problem. It can't be enjoyable for an animal to be in the company of drunk humans crammed into a small space. If the owners really had the well being of their animals in mind they wouldn't bring them into a bar in the first place.

•**DOMESTICS** Even cops are leery of domestic disputes, so a bartender is well advised to move very carefully into this terrain. My first approach, when I see a domestic brewing, is to ignore it and hope it resolves itself peacefully, which it usually does. But once it starts to get out of hand I have to step in. One thing I'm very careful about is not to take a side, no matter what the circumstances. My first move is to tell them to settle down. If they persist I tell them that they have to leave, which they usually do, with a bit of embarrassment. If they don't and their dispute turns violent, other bar patrons will begin to speak up. At this point, in my experience, the couple will move on. **NOTE:** If forced to get physical, be advised that which ever half of the couple you grab, the other half will be on your back.

•**PYROTECHNICS** People like to play with fire. There are bar tricks based on matches and Zippos. People like to burn things and light their drinks on fire. A certain amount of this behavior is to be expected and tolerated, but it's wise to keep it below the level of bonfires.

Firecrackers and stink bombs are as good a reason to expel a patron from a bar as they were to expel a student from grade school, where they most likely developed this hobby.

Lighting fellow customers on fire is considered bad form in most bars.

# Tricksters

•**BARROOM BETS** Spend enough time in a bar and you'll eventually meet someone who will offer to bet you that he or she can do something that you know is impossible. My advice is to never bet more than it's worth to you to see just how this person will accomplish the feat, because you're going to lose.

Generally speaking, these bets will be based on the person's ability to perform seemingly impossible physical acts. Sometimes it's based on a trick, sometimes it's based on ambiguous wording or esoteric knowledge, but no matter how impossible the act seems, I assure you that the person making the claim can do it.

These bets can usually be brought down in price from twenty dollars to a drink to nothing but a challenge. Essentially, these people just want to show you that they know a trick that you don't know, or that they can do something you can't. They'll take your money if you're foolish enough to bet them, but when pushed, and if there are no takers, they will usually perform their little trick for free.

For instance: Don't bet against a guy who claims he can bite his own eye, unless you want to see him pull his glass eye out of his eye socket. And don't bet the same guy that he can't bite his other eye, unless you want to see him remove his dentures and do just that.

•**SUCKER BETS** Though often used interchangeably with *barroom bets*, I define *sucker bets* a bit differently. I see these as more predatory and having less to do with tricks or feats and more to do with cons. They are often based on some sort of information or trivia. As they have little to do with showing off, they almost always involve a bet and the person pushing for the bet definitely wants your money.

A good rule of thumb is not to place bets in bars. For one thing, if you're in a bar you're probably drinking and your mind won't be as clear as it should be for wagering. Men seem to be particularly vulnerable, as alcohol heightens machismo, which makes challenges hard to walk away from. Here, just as with *barroom bets*, if someone claims something is so, no matter how ridiculous and unlikely it seems, you can be sure it probably is so and you will lose your money if you bet.

For instance, would you bet against a guy who claimed that San Francisco has a higher average relative humidity than Washington D.C. or New York City?

•**BAR TRICKS** People who spend a lot of time in bars often amuse themselves and their friends with games, puzzles and tricks that can be played with the things you find around a bar: Napkins, matches, glasses, spoons, knives, etc. Betting usually isn't part of these diversions, and while some are quite boring, others can be ingenious.

The best one I remember was shown to me by a drop-in customer. After a couple of drinks and a bit of conversation with me and a person seated next to her at the bar, she asked me for two highball glasses (they must be of the type depicted in **GLASSWARE** on p166) and a knife. She told me to hold the two glasses underwater in my sink until they were full and there were no air bubbles inside them. Then she told me to put the tops together with the rims aligned and remove them slowly from the sink, one right side-up, the other upside-down. I did so and, due to the vacuum created by the absence of air, the water remained inside the two-part vessel.

She then had me place them on the bar. She put a dime on the top of the two-part vessel (the bottom of the upside-down glass), laid the knife next to the glasses and told me that the object was to get the dime inside the bottom glass without spilling any water from the top glass, and that I could use nothing but the knife to touch the glasses or the dime. I looked at the problem for a while but could think of no solution, and figuring there had to be a trick to it, I gave up and waited to see how she would solve it.

Her first move was to take the knife and gently tap the upper glass until it slid over, ever so slightly. There was now a gap between the rims of the upper and lower glasses. The vacuum inside and/or the surface tension of the water, prevented any of the liquid from leaking out through the thin opening. Then she took the knife and pushed the dime from where it was lying in the center of the upside-down glass to a position where it overhung the edge of the glass, enabling her to slide the knife under the dime. In this way she was able to pick up the dime and lower it into position next to the lip of the lower glass. She turned the knife to the side, which allowed the dime to slide off the knife and through the gap between the rims of the glasses. The dime slid through the water and came to rest in the bottom of the upright glass. She then tapped the upper glass back into place. Problem solved.

•**BARROOM CONS** Never buy jewelry from a guy you meet in a bar no matter how sad his story is, or how much he tries to convince you it's stolen merchandise. It's not stolen. It's fake.

# The Parade of Customers

•**BYOB**ERS Persons who sneak their own booze into the bar. They usually leave their empties underneath their table for the wait staff to clean-up. A.K.A. Thieves.

•**B**AR/**PUB** CRAWLS Similar to a Brodeo except there are generally a few women mixed in. Often they are comprised of co-workers from a large corporation. Participants in this realm often tend to wear something to identify themselves as being part of the group and to exclude outsiders. I suppose this is for safety; they want to know who it's safe to talk to.

•**B**ARGOYLES The stoney faced drunks who stare across the bar at the bartender (i.e. customers).

•**B**ARKERS "The path to hell is paved with good intentions." Occasionally a customer, usually one who is a bit juiced, will go outside to smoke and while there beckon passersby to enter, thinking he's helping by attracting new business. This almost never works in the bartender's favor. The average person, when encountering a drunk in front of a bar who's waving them in, keeps on walking. The ones who do accept such an invitation tend to be trouble makers, who the bartender will then have to deal with.

•**BACHELORETTE PARTIES** Nothing makes the bar staff cringe faster than a group of women wearing tiaras and veils entering their bar.

•**BIG SHOTS** Guys, and it is usually but not always a guy, who insists on paying for the round of drinks, then leaves a stingy tip or nothing at all.

•**BLUE FACED ZOMBIES** Device slaves who spend most or all of their time in a bar staring into a smart phone, their faces glowing blue; they bring nothing to the party.

•**BRO** The post-fraternity type who generally have to wear suits at work. On their days off they show their true selves by all wearing identical outfits. However, instead of the corporate mandated suit, they choose to wear the douche-a-form. They always address one another as, *bro,* hence the name.

•**BRODEO** Five or more (usually more) bros, decked out in their douche-a-forms, out on the town to get drunk and meet women. They enter your bar as a group, presumably with the idea to meet a similar number of like minded women. Or perhaps it's understood that if even one of them finds a woman to talk to, the rest go into wingman mode.

•**BRO-GRAMMER** Bros from the high-tech sector.

•**BRONADO**(Brō•nā•dō) Five or more bros out on the town who enter your bar, order shots, do them quickly, then leave.

•**CAMPERS** People who spend very little money, yet stay in the barroom for hours, using their computer or smart phone, spreading their belongings around, asking for water, electric outlets, using the restrooms, etc.

•**DOUCHE-A-FORM** The Bros preferred uniform: Shorts, T-shirt, flipflops (or tennis shoes or top-siders with no socks), and a baseball cap (worn backwards by the more daring bros).

•**DOUCHEBAG** An odious male customer who doesn't quite reach the level of scumbag. He's the guy who announces, "Let's get this party started!" when he enters.

•**DOUCHETTE** (informal) A female Douchebag. In more formal settings, Douchiatrix is considered proper.

•**Daddy's boy** A guy who addresses the bartender as Chief, Sport, Boss, etc.

•**Daddy's girl** A gal who looks at you like she doesn't understand when you tell her, "No," no matter what her request.

•**Diddliographer** A person who writes about a subject of which he knows diddly.

•**Experts** Persons with a large group who advise the one paying for the round that they are tipping too much.

•**Furniture movers** People who pull bar stools out from the bar, and otherwise rearrange bar furniture, blocking foot traffic to and from the restroom, as well as other areas of the bar, and slows members of the wait staff on their way to the tables. (see *Office Drones*). Also kown as "Road Blockers."

•**Ghosting** The guy who generously orders drinks for his friends and himself, then goes to the restroom. When the drinks arrive he's nowhere to be seen, so the friends are forced to pay. He thinks no one notices his little ploy.

•**Litter bugs** People who litter the bar in front of them with purses, phones, jackets and shopping bags, leaving the bartender nowhere to put the drink.

•**Mr./Ms. double wide** People who put their personal belongings on the bar stool next to the one they're sitting on to give themselves ample space. This is as annoying and rude in a crowded bar as it is on a crowded bus.

•**Mr./Ms. apologetic** A man or woman, usually drunk, who's entire interaction with the bartender consists of apologizing for being such an annoying customer.

•**Office drones** Those persons who live lives of quiet desperation during the week, but on Friday and Saturday nights they enter the bar as a group and act as if they're the only ones in the room. Their calling card is loudness, as if to say, "Look at me. Look at me. I'm out having fun, not stuck at work." They also tend to be furniture movers, so they can form a tight knit, inward looking group. As other customers are forced to squeeze past them they respond with annoyed glances or simply act oblivious.

•**Princes and princesses** People who believe the world revolves around them and their desires. Bartenders do these people a valuable service by divesting them of their delusion, a service that should have been provided by their parents.

•**Quarters** A game played by douches who throw quarters down on the table top in an attempt to bounce them into a rocks glass, making a loud, annoying racket in the process. Luckily this game has gone out of style, probably because the douchery who used to play it got yelled at to, "Cut it out!" by bar staff every time they did.

•**"Racist!"** This accusation always comes from some drunk who would have been cut off sooner and been given even less respect by a bartender of their own race/ethnicity.

•**Rear guard** Persons with a large group who lag behind, then scoop up tips left by someone else in their group. A.K.A. Thieves.

•**Scumbag** A low, vile individual not above stealing and/or other misdemeanors.

•**Shit-show** A bar, or anywhere, where all hell is breaking lose, generally caused by having a high percentage of those on this list in attendance.

•**Shit-storm** A shit-show made up of over fifty percent of characters from this list (e.g. St. Patrick's Day).

•**A Perfect Shit-storm** Thankfully, these are quite rare. It occurs when nearly the entire population of the barroom is made up of characters from this list (e.g. Santa-Con).

•**Short arms** The guy who orders drinks but can't reach his wallet. Ever. I guess he figures the bartender will forget or his companions will pick up the tab.

•**Sidler/Creeper** A guy who lurks in barroom, then moves to sit next to any female customer who enters alone.

•**Singers** Any customer or group of customers who sings or chants anything out loud, other than Happy Birthday.

•**Slammers** Large groups showing up without a heads-up. Of course you want the business, but getting hit all at once by a group of twenty or more individuals, without any previous notice can put you in the weeds before you know what hit you.

•**TAP YOUR PLINY** To mastubate.

•**TECHNO-TOOLS** A person who is bowled over by technology and uses it in inappropriate or counterproductive ways to the point that they become a social outcast due to their obsession.

•**TEENAGERS** Customers who clap when someone breaks a glass.

•**TIP THIEVES** Persons who hover at the bar, then scoop up tips when they think no one is watching. A.K.A. Scumbags.

•**WASTERS** Customers who spill drinks, then grab a ginormous wad of serviettes to wipe it up, rather than use a bar rag.

•**WHITE KNIGHT** A guy who jumps up to protect a woman in distress with the intention of scoring points and ending up in the sack with her.

•**YAHOOS** People who feel they have to yell, *Ya-hooo!* (or anything similar) to call attention to the fact they are out drinking in a bar.

•**YELP** The sound a puppy makes when you step on its tail.

•**YELPERS** Persons who say nothing at the bar, but post a complaint at an on-line snitch-site, outlining the perceived slight they experienced, showing the world what a discriminating and sophisticated patron they are. A.K.A. Cowardly Snitches.

# Bar Terms

•**86'D** Bar terminology for a person who is no longer allowed on the premises. It also refers to an item that has run out and for which there is no replacement. For instance, if a keg of beer blows and there is no backup keg, that beer is said to be 86'd.

•**12 YEAR OLD** A person who looks 21 or younger.

•**A.B.C.** Alcoholic Beverage Control. This is what it's called in California, it's probably called different things in different states, but they all have some version of it. They check on bars to see if they are complying with state laws concerning the sale and consumption of alcohol.

•**ATTITUDE ADJUSTMENT** A shot of alcohol a bartender takes at the beginning of his shift or when he's about to get slammed, to get in the mood (see *Personality Juice*).

•**BACK-BAR** The large fixture against the wall behind the bar where the call and top-shelf booze, the glassware and the cash register are kept. They range from simple and utilitarian to extremely ornate. The ornate ones are highly prized and will often be bought from old bars that are going out of business to do service in a bar that's being built or remodeled.

•**BANK** The bank is the cash given to the bartender at the beginning of his shift in order to make change. This beginning amount will vary greatly from one bar to the next. At the end of the shift it is removed from the cash in the till and put aside for the next days shift (see *Drop*).

•**BAR-BACK** Someone who works with the bartender, but doesn't usually make drinks. Their duties include bussing glassware, getting ice, washing glassware, restocking beer, etc.

•**BAR SCORE** Something lost in the bar and not claimed that the bartender takes for his own.

•**BEER TOWER** The fixtures protruding from the bar where the taps are clustered.

•**BREAKAGE** The bottles of booze emptied during the course of a shift. The expression comes from the act of breaking a bottle when it was emptied, which was the law until several decades ago. Some bars had a steel rod affixed to the bar to facilitate breaking the neck of the bottle. This is no longer required, but the name endures.

•**BRUISING THE GIN** To shake the ice and gin violently when making a martini. This causes the gin to become diluted, produces ice chips, dissipates the fragrance and can cause the gin to become cloudy for a few moments by introducing air into the gin. This is why those who drink gin martinis prefer them stirred, rather than shaken (see *Stirred vs. Shaken*).

•**BUILT DRINK** A drink that takes extra work to produce, such as coffee drinks, Bloody Marys, Margaritas and up-drinks.

•**BUMP OR UP-CHARGE** An extra charge for drinks that call for a martini pour or that have to be built.

•**BURIED** A stronger expression for *in the weeds*.

•**BUSSER** Someone who carries the empty glassware from the tables back to the bar. In large clubs or restaurants it's someone whose sole duties are bussing. In smaller establishments it's the bar-back and/or the waiter. In very small bars it's the bartender. Occasionally it's a customer.

•**BUYBACK** A free drink after buying a certain number. Some bars use buyback chips to keep track of when each customer is due his freebie. Not all bars offer buybacks and many that do, do so during Happy Hours only.

•**CALL** These are the moderately priced name brands. They are a step up from well. They are usually found behind the bartender, in the lower shelves of the back-bar. They're called *call* because you must specify or call them by name. Otherwise, you'll get well booze.

•**CARRYING (A CO-WORKER)** If one bartender does all of the work while his co-worker stands chatting with friends or an attractive customer the first bartender is said to be carrying the other. Of course, this is often a matter of perception.

•**COUNT** To pour a shot of booze accurately the bartender counts in her head to time her pour. Most bartenders count to four, some count to three or five. For drinks that require more than a shot of booze or when making several drinks at once, they count higher. For instance, I count four for a shot. When making a martini I count five. If I'm making two martinis in the same mixing vessel, I count ten.

•**DASH** This is the smallest amount in a drink recipe. Generally, it comes from a bottle with a tiny hole in the top, such as bitters. To pour a dash the bartender takes the bottle and turns it over so about one drop comes out.

•**DOUBLE** Two shots.

•**DROP, THE** The drop is the money left over after the bank is removed, in other words, the day's gross. It's called *the drop* because it's often dropped through a slot in the safe.

•**FLOAT** Booze added last and allowed to float on top of the drink. Roughly equal to a one count.

•**FLUFF THE CHANGE** Break it down into smaller denominations.

•**FREE POUR** Poured straight from the bottle using no measuring device or pour spout.

•**GIVING THE HOUSE AWAY** Giving away too many free drinks.

•**GOLDEN HANDCUFFS** A reference to how few people are able to get out of the bar business once they're in. Some do make it but they often come snooping around for, "Just one or two shifts a week," a year or so after they thought they were out.

•**GUN, THE** A hose with a multi-buttoned nozzle for dispensing mixers such as cola, tonic, water, etc. It's used because it's faster, cheaper and easier than using bottled mixers.

•**HAPPY HOUR(S)** The time of day when business is slow. It's used to attract business into the bar during these slow periods, typically late afternoon to early evening.

•**HEAD MELTER** A customer who drones on incessantly about trivial or otherwise uninteresting topics.

•**HEAVY HAND** A bartender who pours well over a normal shot.

•**HIGHBALL** These are the mixed drinks most often ordered and consist of one shot of booze over ice in a highball glass filled with the appropriate mixer. Examples of highballs are, Gin and Tonic, Cape Cod, Rum and Coke, etc.

•**HOPSTER** Another term for a beer snob.

•**HOVERING** When space is at a premium, customers who have yet to find a seat will position themselves near customers who appear to be ready to leave in hopes of snagging their bar stool or table. This can become annoying to both parties; those about to leave who feel they are being rushed and to those doing the hovering who begin to suspect that their targets are consciously moving slowly out of spite.

•**ICE WELL** This is the sink-like bin that the ice is kept in.

•**IDIOT TAX** An extra charge a bartender surreptitiously adds to the price of drinks when dealing with stiffs and/or other annoying/problematic customers.

•**INDUSTRY, THE** The bar and restaurant industry.

•**INDUSTRY COURTESY** Freebees offered to other members of The Industry.

•**INDUSTRY NIGHT** A night of the week, highly coveted by bartenders, when many off-duty members of The Industry are present.

•**IN THE WEEDS** When the customers' demand for drinks exceeds the bar staff's ability to supply them.

•**IT'S MY FRIDAY NIGHT** An expression commonly used by bar staff to denote the day before one to several days off, no matter what day it is in the *real world*.

•**LONG POUR (OR MARTINI POUR)** Approximately ½ oz. more than a regular pour.

•**Matts** The rubber matts on the floor behind the bar that the bar staff walks on. They are mandated by law because the floor behind the bar is usually cement or tile. Working on such a floor is slippery when wet and, since it's a hard surface, can lead to leg injuries after working on it for a few years. In the old days it was made of wooden planks, sometimes attached to rubber strips so that it could be rolled up. (see *Plank, The*)

•**Bar matt** The long, narrow rubber matts in front of the bartender's work station where he places the glass in which he's making a drink. They have a textured surface which makes the glass less likely to be knocked over and it collects the spillage in its textured surface.

•**Matt shot** A foul drink made by holding the bar matt over a glass, bending the matt in the middle and allowing the collected spillage to pour into the glass: gin, tomato juice, cream, bourbon, red wine, Fernet, what ever has missed the glass. Yeah sure, I've drank a few over the years.

•**Neat** This is how you order when you want booze straight from the bottle into your glass with no other modification and no ice. You can also say straight, but not *straight-up*, which means chilled and strained into an *up* or *martini glass*.

•**Nervous glass** This refers to the practice of serving a drink in the next larger sized glass. For instance, a neat shot of booze in a rocks glass rather than a shot glass. The expression is a reference to drinkers with the nervous habit of swirling or jiggling their drink between taking sips.

•**One-count** Approximately one quarter of a shot.

•**One on the cuff** A free drink.

•**Over served** This is said to occur when a bartender serves a person who has reached the tipping point in terms of inebriation.

•**Personality juice** A shot of alcohol the bartender takes to make him more jovial and out-going when he's feeling anything but.

•**Plank, The** Slang for the bar. In the Middle Ages when a woman's batch of home brew was ready for consumption, she would arrange two barrels with a plank of wood spanning the gulf between them, on which to serve her neighbors. **Also:** In the old days when the matt behind the bar was made of wooden planks, bartending was sometimes referred to as, "Walking the planks."

•**PONY SHOT** One ounce of booze.

•**POUR COST** Pour cost refers to the cost of booze per drink, or to put it another way; how many shots the bar gets out of a bottle. Some bar owners (usually corporate owners) are very strict about their pour costs and will berate the bartenders if they find the pour cost rising above a certain percentage of sales, usually around 20%.

•**PREEMPTIVE DRINKING** Drinking in the afternoon to get it over with early, thus avoiding having to drink at night—Drinking in the afternoon is cheaper and you encounter a better class of drunk.

•**PRODUCT ANALYSIS** What a bartender calls drinking on the job.

•**PROOF** One-half of one percent of alcohol. Eighty-proof booze is forty percent alcohol.

•**PTSD** Post Traumatic Santa-con Disorder. The feelings of dread, anger and disgust you get, after working a Santa-con shift, when you see someone dressed in any part of a Santa costume. It usually persists until after Xmas (this one was coined by Joanna Lioce).

•**RING** Total sales for a shift. It's called the ring because of the sound registers make when sales are registered, *Ka-ching!*

•**ROCKS/OVER** This means a shot of booze in a glass filled with ice.

•**SHOT OR JIGGER** One-and-a-half to two ounces of booze.

•**SHRINKAGE 1)** Inventory that is lost, destroyed, stolen, broken, etc. **2)** The effect swimming in cold water has upon male genitalia.

•**SLAMMED** When the customers' demand for drinks equals the bar staff's ability to supply them. It also refers to a large group entering the barroom at once, causing the bar staff to shift into high gear.

•**SPANKED** To have worked a grueling bar shift.

•**SPEED POUR** Using bottles fitted with pour spouts, bartenders count in their heads at a regular rate to time their pour. It's faster than measuring with a shot glass and more accurate than free pouring.

•**SPEED WELL OR SPEED RACK** This is the rack attached to the ice well. The bartender stands behind it and is thus able to scoop ice into a glass and quickly grab a bottle from the well to produce a drink.

•**SPLASH** This means a shot of booze and a tiny amount of whatever you specify, for instance, "scotch with a splash of water," "gin with a splash of tonic," or "vodka-soda with a splash of cranberry." It's used for mixers which are on the gun or in a bottle that don't take a speed-pour spout. These mixers can't be poured as accurately as booze from a speed-pour spout. A splash is roughly equivalent to a two-count.

•**STIFF (STIFFED)** A customer who doesn't tip (to serve a customer and receive no tip).

•**STIRRED VS. SHAKEN** The two ways booze is chilled. Both begin by putting ice into a mixing vessel and then adding booze. Then the bartender either stirs it with a long handled spoon or covers the mixing vessel and shakes it. Both methods chill the booze, and if it's a drink with two or more ingredients, mix them. Shaking is the more violent method and will generally make the booze colder quicker but will also dilute the drink more and often leave ice chips in the finished drink. In the case of gin it can also dissipate some of the fragrance and cause it to become temporarily cloudy. This is known as bruising the gin, which is why some martini aficionados insist on stirred martinis. For similar reasons Manhattans are also usually stirred. Personally, I never stir or shake martinis, I swirl them.

•**TALL** When you order a drink tall you get the same amount of booze, but you get it in a Collins glass. The extra space in the glass is taken up by mixer, not by booze. You should order your drink tall if you want it to be more diluted. If you want it less diluted, you should order it with a splash. If you want more booze you should order a double.

•**TIP-OUT** A percent of your tips that you give to another worker, such as the tip-out waiters give to the bartender. The reason for tip-outs, as with most things in a bar, is the smooth operation of the bar. A bartender isn't as likely to react quickly when a server orders a drink from him if there isn't something waiting for him when the dust settles. Just as with stingy customers, a member of the wait staff that scrimps on the tip-out will find that he or she isn't getting top priority from the bartenders.

- **TOP-SHELF/PREMIUM** These are the priciest offerings. They are called top-shelf because they are usually found on the top shelves of the back-bar.

- **TRAINING WHEELS** The salt and lime some people take with tequila.

- **UP/STRAIGHT-UP** This means chilled over ice (stirred or shaken), then strained into a glass, generally a chilled up glass.

- **VIRGIN** A drink without booze, for instance, a virgin Bloody Mary: tomato juice and all the ingredients and garnishes but no vodka.

- **WALK WITH** How much a bar worker made after tipping-out (i.e. How much they walked out the door with).

- **WELL/HOUSE BRANDS** The entry-level booze, the cheap stuff you get if you don't order a name brand. They're called *well* because they're kept in the speed well. They're called *house brands* in upscale bars.

- **WILTED DRINKS** Drinks are said to be wilted when they pass their peak in terms of flavor. Up drinks wilt the fastest; that is, they become warmer than is preferred. For instance, a gin martini is only good for about twenty minutes after it's been made. Over drinks last a good deal longer; they are considered wilted when the ice has melted enough to dilute the drink past what is preferable. Beer wilts when it sits so long as to become too warm to drink.

- **X** A running total of sales rung into the register since it was last Zee'd.

- **Z (Z-OUT)** The final tally of sales rung into the register during a shift, which also clears all sales so the register is ready to begin a new tally.

# Travel is the purest form of conspicuous consumption.

# Common types of glassware

# Glassware

N̲OT ALL BARS HAVE A FULL COMPLEMENT of glassware. Many will put one type of glass to two or more uses. The reasons for this are:

**1) COST** It costs more to have more types of glassware.

**2) SPACE** There often isn't enough space to have all the different types of glassware called for by the writers of bar guides. Usually a bar will have the most room behind the bar allotted to the types of glassware it uses most: rocks, highball and beer glasses, for instance. Infrequently used glassware must fit into the remaining space. If there isn't room for a type that is almost never needed, the bar will choose to do without and press another type of glass into service when the need arises.

THE COMMON TYPES OF GLASSWARE FOUND IN A BAR ARE:

•**SHOT GLASS** These are the smallest glasses in the bar. They are not all the same size, but on average they hold 2 oz. with a cap line indicating 1.0 oz.

•**ROCKS** This is the little glass, generally holding four ounces, that you get when ordering booze on the rocks or neat. These are generally faceted and measure 2 oz. when filled to the top of the facets.

•**HIGHBALL** These glasses look like rocks glasses only larger (six or eight ounces). There are several basic variations on the Highball, the two most common are those with faceted sides and those with straight sides.

•**TALL** (also called Collins, Chimney, Zombie or Bucket). Other than the Bucket, these are the glasses any drink ordered *tall* comes in. The Bucket holds roughly the same amount, usually 10 or 12 ounces, but is squat and wide rather than tall and thin.

•**PINT** The biggest glass in most bars, used for serving tap beer. In bars that use a narrow range of glassware these are used for drinks served tall. The standard size is 16 oz.

•**PILSNER** Slender, tapered beer glass with a heavy footing. Standard size is 8 0z.

•**MARTINI** These are the inverted cones with stems in which drinks are served up. These have no standard size, some are tiny, others huge. One thing to remember is that they are inverted cones, and as such each ascending section will hold more than the lower one; a tiny martini glass filled to the top will hold as much as a huge one that is half full.

•**CHAMPAGNE FLUTE** These are the glasses that champagne is served in. They are shaped like long, thin, tapered cylinders and are stemmed.

•**WINE GLASS** Rounded sides, stemmed.

•**SNIFTER** Squat, round, stemmed. For cognac, single-malt scotch, aged rum, etc.